A PRACTICAL GUIDE TO CHILD DEVELOPMENT

Volume 2 The Family

Valda Reynolds Cert. Ed.
Joint Chief Examiner, Midland Examining Group, for GCSE Home Economics:
Child Development

Stanley Thornes (Publishers) Ltd

First published in 1987 by
Stanley Thornes (Publishers) Ltd
Old Station Drive
Leckhampton
CHELTENHAM GL53 0DN
England

Reprinted 1988 (twice)
Reprinted 1990

British Library Cataloguing in Publication Data

Reynolds, Valda
    A practical guide to child development.
    Vol. 2: The Family
    1.   Child development
    I.   Title
    155.4   BF721

    ISBN 0–85950–240–6

Typeset by Tech-Set, Gateshead, Tyne & Wear
Printed and bound in Great Britain at The Bath Press, Avon

Contents

Preface

The information in this book complements that contained in Volume 1.

Ideally the care and development of a child should be placed within the context of a loving, caring family background. All too often this is not achieved; not because of lack of finance but because of lack of knowledge, common sense and motivation. Family structure and family circumstances change but parental responsibilities do not change. Many families today have special needs, and experience the problems of modern living. Community care and provision cater for some of these needs, but not always satisfactorily.

The four main sections of this book deal with important aspects of family life which affect the developing child (referred to as 'he' or 'she' in alternate chapters), and the social changes which are taking place in these; the place of the family in society, and the problems and conditions within our society which affect this; the needs and care of children with special needs and their families; and the nature of the help available from the State and from voluntary agencies for all families.

The main part of each section ends with a summary and evaluation. The follow-up work in each section includes fact finding exercises, data response and problem solving exercises, and free response questions. Activities and suggestions for discussion test the practical and communication skills of pupils.

Four appendices provide suggestions for further reading; an example of a structured examination question with mark allocation and marking guidelines; helpful information about, and suggestions for, internally assessed coursework for GCSE; and assessment objectives for each section. There is a selective glossary.

The statistical information is as up-to-date as possible, but as some figures change yearly, constant updating is needed.

This book can be used independently or in conjunction with Volume 1 to supply the information required in GCSE Home Economics: Child Development or Home and Family syllabuses, and gives some basic sociology work. The depth and range of information is sufficient to stretch the able pupil and stimulate those of lower ability.

These volumes provide a text which is closely related to the philosophy and ideals set out in the national criteria for GCSE.

Valda Reynolds
1987

Acknowledgements

The author and publishers would like to thank the following for their help in the production of this book:

Pam Knight for the cover design.
Margaret Lanfear for typing the script.
Peter Reynolds for compiling the index, research and script checking.

We would like to thank the following for permission to reproduce previously published material:

Encyclopaedia Britannica, Inc.
Milupa Limited.
the Controller of HMSO.

We would like to thank the following for prints and permission to reproduce them:

Adrian Rowland (pp. 59, 71).
ASBAH (p. 88). The picture is of Derek Griffin and was taken by his father, Howard Griffin.
BBC Hulton Picture Library (pp. 13, 41).
John R. Simmons (p. 57).
John Sturrock/Network (p. 71).
Martin West (pp. 55, 67).
Mike Abrahams/Network (p. 36).
Mike Yardley MCSD (p. 37).
National Children's Home (pp. 55, 57, 59, 67, 71).
NSPCC (p. 59).
RNIB (pp. 89, 115, 120).
Steve Benbow/Network (p. 59).
Tony Stone Worldwide (p. 2).

Every effort has been made to contact copyright holders, but we apologise if any have been overlooked.

SECTION A **The Family in Society**

1 Family Structures

The extended and the nuclear family

In a 1984 survey, over a thousand people were asked this question:

> Some people think of the typical household in Britain as consisting of a husband, a wife and two or three children. Do you believe this is what the typical household consists of or not?

79 per cent answered yes, 17 per cent answered no, and 4 per cent didn't know. In fact, only a small proportion of households (about 14 per cent) consists of the type of family shown in the photograph, and most of today's family units are made up in many different forms.

The gradual decline, from the beginning of this century, of the **extended family** – the structure made up of several generations of the family all living together or close by – resulted in the sort of **nuclear** or **conjugal family** shown here becoming the typical structure. Gradually, mainly since the 1950s and 60s, the family structure in Britain has been changing yet again to give many different patterns of family life.

Factors which contributed towards the decline of the extended family and the development of the nuclear family include the following:

- As society became more industrialised, people needed to travel further to get to their work places and family units split up into smaller groups.
- More workers were better paid and could afford to set up their own homes when they married.

- State education meant that people became more knowledgeable about ways of life other than their own, and tended to want a better standard of living.

- As women became better educated and had more opportunities to work, they tended to gain greater independence. Often they were not happy to be one of a large family group when they married, but wished to set up homes of their own.

- Better and quicker forms of transport, such as trains, cars and buses, became more widely available, and families could keep in contact even when living apart.

- The old concepts of living in large family houses in built-up areas gradually began to change. The smaller families moved to smaller units on modern estates.

- More efficient methods of family planning meant that people could choose when to have children and the number they wanted. The large Victorian-type family became less common. By 1961 only 8 per cent of married couples had three or more dependent children, and by 1983 only 6 per cent had three or more dependent children.

Other family structures

Single father family

Single mother family

Nuclear family

Adoptive family

No children family

Types of family structure

Make a note of all the family structures that appear in TV programmes during one week. How many of the above are shown? Does this give a true picture of British family life?

Because of ever-changing social circumstances and values, the nuclear family of father, mother and one or two children is no longer the typical structure. The modern family structure may be any one of the following:

- a couple without children. An increasing proportion of modern couples opt not to have children. In 1986, 32 per cent of married couples had no children.

- a couple with one dependent child or more. In 1986, 45 per cent of households came into this category.

- a parent or parents with one or more adopted or foster children. The number of adoptions in Britain in 1983 was 10 000. This compares with 23 000 in 1971, showing a steady downward trend (apart from 1982 when there was a 3 per cent rise) during the last decade. This is largely due to the fact that fewer babies are available for adoption, because there are fewer unwanted pregnancies, and single parents are now more able to support their babies.

- a lone parent (male or female) with one child or more, left on his or her own after divorce, separation or the death of a partner: usually known as the **lone-parent** or **single-parent family**. There were 70 per cent more single-parent families in 1982 than there had been ten years earlier. By 1985, 14 per cent of all families with dependent children were headed by a lone parent.

- an unmarried woman with one child or more.

- an unmarried couple with a permanent relationship, with one child or more.

- couples living together with adopted or fostered children, or with children conceived by artificial insemination.

Social statistics

On the next two pages there are charts and tables showing statistics on family changes.

Look at the first chart on p. 5.

How many women are separated by divorce?

How many unmarried mothers are there?

What is the total number of lone mothers?

What is the total number of lone fathers?

Suggest some of the reasons for the sharp difference in numbers between lone mothers and lone fathers.

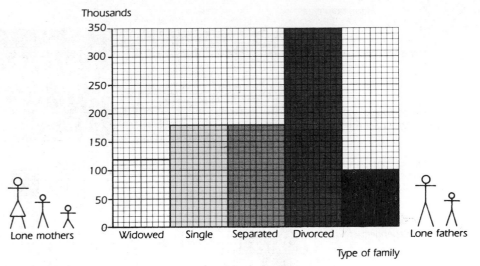

Single-parent families

Only one block is shown for lone fathers because the number is too small to be broken down into different categories.

Source: *Hansard 1985*

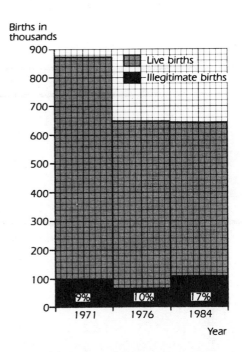

Percentage of illegitimate births, 1971–84

Source: *Social Trends 1985*

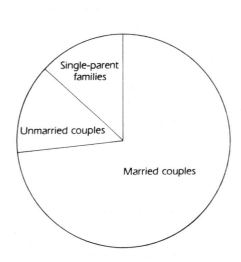

Families with dependent children, 1982

Source: *General Household Survey 1981–3*

Household type

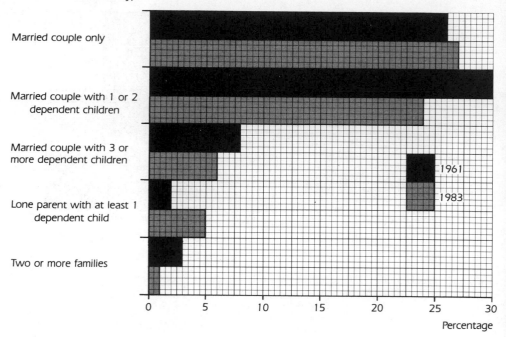

Households by type

Source: *Social Trends 1985*

Households by size

	1961	1971	1981	1983
	%	%	%	%
1 person	12	18	22	23
2 people	30	32	32	32
3 people	23	19	17	17
4 people	19	17	18	18
5 people	9	8	7	7
6 or more people	7	6	4	3
Average household size	3.09	2.89	2.71	2.64

Source: *Social Trends 1985*

2 Changes in Family Structures

Causes

These changes in family structures have been brought about by social changes, which include:

- **Development of the Welfare State**   The State has gradually taken over some of the responsibilities of family life. It now provides financial, material and personal help for many families and individuals who need it.

- **Changing role of women**   This has led to changing roles within the family. The traditional role of upper working-class and middle-class women was to marry and remain in the home to look after the family. The two world wars made it necessary for women to take the place of men in the work force. This, plus more enlightened education and social acceptance, encouraged women to take the dual roles of home maker and second or only breadwinner. At first many women went out to work to buy luxuries for their family and upgrade their standard of living, and some pursued a professional career. Gradually it became common for women to continue with their jobs when they married, take maternity leave when they became pregnant, and return to work after the baby was born. Men began, from necessity, to help with looking after the children and the household chores. With the problems which unemployment has brought, role reversals within the family have become less unusual, with the woman going out to work, and the man looking after the home.

Busdriver

Electrician

Nanny

Roadworker

Train driver

Jockey

Home Economics teacher

Bank manager

Optician

Secretary

Midwife

Newspaper editor

Traditional male and female jobs

Which of the illustrations on the previous page are traditionally female jobs and which are traditionally male?

Do you think that it is fair that many of the top jobs go to men?

Why do you think that the jobs shown on p. 7 can so easily be divided into traditionally male and female occupations?

What can women do to ensure that they will be considered for traditionally male jobs?

Carry out the following survey among your female schoolfriends and relations.

Name	**Age**	
Questions		**Answers**
1 *What job(s) would you most like to do?*		
2 *Would you prefer to do a traditionally female job or would you like to try a traditionally male job?*		
3 *What type of training are you willing to undertake?*		
4 *Would you mind being the only female on a course traditionally intended mainly for males?*		
5 *If you were a trained bus driver/jockey/electrician, would you give up work to bring up your family?*		
6 *Would you mind being married to a man who worked as a midwife?*		
7 *Would your parents mind if you told them you wanted to work in a garage?*		
8 *Is there anyone in your family who works in a non-traditional male/female job?*		
9 *Do you know any families where mum goes out to work and dad looks after the home and family? Give details.*		
10 *Would you expect to receive the same wage as a man if you were a firefighter?*		

Re-do this questionnaire to make it suitable for giving to a male. Then assess and evaluate the results of your survey.

● **Rise in the divorce rate**   This remained quite low until the end of the Second World War, but by 1983 the UK rate was one of the highest in Europe. This is partly because legislation has made it easier to obtain a divorce. The Divorce Reform Act was passed in 1969, and came into operation in 1971. This made it possible for most couples to divorce if they wished. If the spouses have lived apart for five years, a divorce is obtainable even if one spouse does not want it. This Act plus the availability of Legal Aid has contributed to the steep increase in divorce over the past decade.

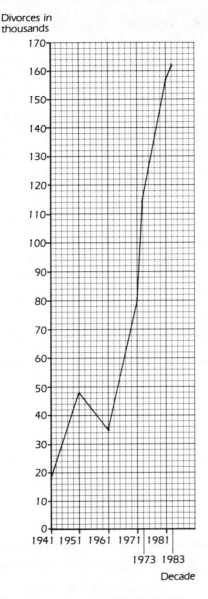

Divorces in thousands

1941 1951 1961 1971 1981
1973 1983
Decade

Divorce rate in the UK, 1941–83

Source: *Social Trends 1985*

What do the figures show from 1941–51?

What is the figure for 1961?

What happens to the rate between 1951 and 1961?

How much rise was there between 1973 and 1983?

Find out if there has been an increase or a decrease in the divorce rate since 1983.

In 1983, almost 50 per cent of all divorces happened within the first ten years of marriage, and over 20 per cent before the fifth wedding anniversary. The total number of children with parents who were divorced was 155 000; 44 000 of these children were under five. The divorce rate was highest for those families where the husband was unemployed, about double the normal rate.

In 1985, there was an 11 per cent increase in divorces in the UK, with 175 000 decrees absolute.

In 1982, 13 per cent of divorces were in marriages where the husband was under 20, and 37 per cent where the wife was under 20. Couples who marry in their teens are twice as likely to divorce as older people.

More than one third of divorcees remarry, but there is a higher rate of divorce among second marriages than among first marriages.

- **Better contraception**   More efficient and widely available contraception, and better contraceptive advice, have contributed to a drop in the birth rate. (See the graph on percentage of illegitimate births, p. 5.)

- **Legalisation of abortion**   (Abortion is termination of pregnancy before the 28th week.) This is also partly responsible for the drop in the birth rate. Abortion was legalised under the Abortion Act (1967), provided there is a risk that the continuance of the pregnancy would injure the mother's life mentally or physically, or that the child would be born seriously handicapped.

Legal abortions performed on women resident in England and Wales, 1969–83

	1969	1971	1979	1981	1983
Marital status and no. of previous children*	%	%	%	%	%
Single women, no children	39	42	46	46	48
Married women, no children	2	3	5	4	4
Married women, 1–3 children	29	30	27	25	23
Widowed, divorced and separated women	9	9	12	13	12
Age of women	(in thousands)				
Under 20 years	9	20	33	35	35
20–34 years	30	56	69	75	74

*For 1969–79 'previous children' includes only those which were live born; from 1981 previous stillborn children are also included.

Source: *Office of Population Censuses and Surveys*

In 1983, there were 127 000 legal abortions to women resident in England and Wales. Over a quarter of these were carried out on girls under 20.

In 1982, 88 per cent of legal abortions were carried out because of possible risk, physical or mental, to the mother, and up to 2 per cent because of risk to the child. Some of these risks are due to the effects of the pregnant woman having rubella (German measles). Other abortions were carried out for social reasons.

- **Break up of large family groups**   During the 1970s and 1980s there has been a movement of population from the large urban areas to smaller towns or rural areas.

About 18 million people, or one third of the population, live in the places shown here. These seven areas are called conurbations – *continuous built-up areas.*

About 25 million people, or one half of the population, live in other urban areas.

About 13 million people, or nearly one fifth of the population, live in rural areas.

Draw a pie chart to illustrate these figures.

In 1981, nearly 90 per cent of the population of England lived in urban areas. Between 1971 and 1981, numbers living in smaller urban areas increased by 10 per cent and the numbers living in rural areas increased by 5 per cent. The building of 'new towns' such as Milton Keynes has drawn families from the densely populated towns. A large proportion of the population of towns such as Liverpool have moved to new housing estates on the outskirts of the towns or into rural developments. This has meant that large family groups who lived near each other and worked together have been broken up into small isolated family units.

- **Media images of the family**   The mass media, which include television, radio, magazines and newspapers, have all contributed to giving some false impressions of family life. Many programmes suggest that divorce, illegitimacy, living together in an unmarried state, etc. are now the norm. In fact, according to government figures in 1983, 90 per cent of people of marriageable age do get married, nine out of ten married couples have children, two out of three marriages survive, and eight out of ten children live with both natural parents.

The pressure of advertising means that material possessions are given more importance than the quality of family life by the media.

All these factors have led to many changes in family life, and also brought about a lot of family problems.

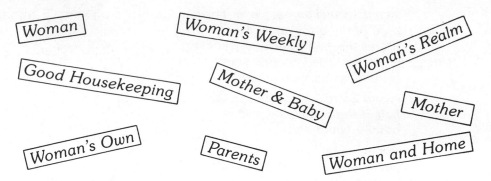

These are all magazines which are aimed at the female market, and cover topics which mainly interest women.

Some of the features which could be included in a magazine aimed at the lone father are:

> *cooking for your under fives*
> *how to choose a babysitter*
> *family finance*
> *choosing the right cleaning agents*
> *improving your social life*
> *your Social Security rights*
> *problem page*

Add to this list and write articles on three of the topics.
Do you think a magazine like this would sell?

Effects

The effects on children and their parents of the changing circumstances of the past decade can be seen in many areas.

Housing and environment

It was not until the end of the nineteenth century that the State became involved with housing. Houses were mainly owned by private landlords, and housing in the big cities was largely overcrowded, insanitary and dangerous. In 1890, 90 per cent of houses were rented from private landlords, and the remaining 10 per cent were owner-occupied.

The Local Authorities were forced into doing something by the appalling slum conditions, and by 1970, 30 per cent of rented accommodation was council housing. In the post-war years there was a big housing shortage and the government undertook an extensive building programme, demolishing slums and replacing them with well-built council houses to be let at a subsidised rent. The stigma attached to council housing gradually disappeared and council houses were built for all classes of the population.

Slums in Glasgow, 1956

Housing conditions generally over the past forty years have improved: there are fewer slums and less overcrowding; many houses are in better condition and contain more modern amenities. As society has become more affluent the tendency has been to want home ownership, and with government encouragement, some people are now buying their own council houses.

The chart that follows shows how private ownership is increasing. (In 1986, home ownership had risen to 63 per cent of households, compared with 33 per cent 30 years earlier.) It also shows how the UK compares with two other wealthy countries.

Housing, 1890–1981

		Rented %		Private ownership %	Other circumstances *(vacant dwellings collectively owned)* %
UK	1890	90		10	
	1970	{20 30	*private council*	50	
	1981	40.3		51.1	8.6
USA	1981	33.0		59.7	7.3
Australia	1981	22.6		61.6	15.8

Source: *Britannica World Data, 1987*

13

Overcrowding in the large cities has been lessened by slum clearance programmes, by building modern estates on the outskirts of towns, and by building specially planned 'new towns' such as Milton Keynes, Stevenage, Telford, etc.

These better housing conditions have improved the quality of life for many families, which shows in better health and less stress, but some problems have also been created. These include:

- breaking up of family groupings, causing loneliness to the young families who move away and to the older people left behind.
- lack of support, and traditions not being passed on from one generation to the next.
- difficulty with community spirit in new towns. They tend to be impersonal and lacking in attractions for young people, and their predominantly young population gives a lack of balance.
- long journeys from home to centres of work mean longer periods of family separation from the family earner.
- financial difficulties caused by high house repayments.
- problems caused to families with young children and the elderly from living in high rise flats (now being replaced). These problems include loneliness, vandalism, damage to lifts, being unable to get out, having nowhere to play, etc.

Relaxed social attitudes

We have a familiar picture of the traditional Victorian family: well disciplined, with father at the head and the children brought up to be 'seen and not heard'. The present situation is very different; two world wars meant that father went away to fight and mother brought up the family single handed, often doing war work at the same time.

In the post-war years the old disciplined family regime never returned, the dual standards of Victorian morality declined and a much more tolerant attitude emerged. This has not necessarily brought about a better society. Less strict discipline at home and at school, a drift away from religious guidance, a change in moral standards, and increasing pressures from the media, have resulted in some cases in:

- a higher proportion of broken homes, and higher rates of abortion, divorce and illegitimacy.
- more child neglect and abuse.
- more cases of vandalism and petty crime, especially amongst young people.
- increasing drug abuse, alcoholism and sexually related diseases.
- the gradual erosion of traditional family values.

Children thrive better and feel happier when given the security of gentle but firm and consistent discipline.

Single-parent and step families

In 1985, Britain had at least one million one-parent families, a 70 per cent increase from ten years earlier. We tend to think of the single-parent family as being of this age, but there have been one-parent families throughout history. There is also a tendency to think of the one-parent family as being a problem family, needing a lot of community support.

There is no reason, though, why children coming from a one-parent family should not be just as happy, well adjusted and socially acceptable as any other children, and they usually are. However, a single parent may have a greater proportion of difficulties to face than a family where there are two parents, and these difficulties can affect the children. Such difficulties include:

- **financial problems**   Almost 50 per cent of families on income support are single-parent families. The main sources of income for the one-parent family are: earnings, maintenance, income support, widows' benefit or private income.

  As about 90 per cent of single parents are women, they often have difficulty finding suitable jobs, and their earnings may be lower than a man's. Maintenance payments (from the father or ex-husband) may be irregular or non-existent. State benefits are very confusing to some people; they either do not know they are entitled to them, or do not know how to claim them – every year about one quarter of supplementary benefits remain unclaimed by those who are entitled to them. Very few one-parent families have private means.

  This means that these families can suffer financial hardships. A useful organisation dealing with these problems is

  One Parent Families, 255 Kentish Town Road, London NW5 2LX.

  They provide free confidential advice for one-parent families on housing, finance, family problems, law, taxation, employment, etc. They publish 'Single and Pregnant – A Guide to Benefits'.

- **social attitudes**   Society is still geared towards the two-parent family and attitudes have been slow to change towards the single parent. There may still be a slight stigma attached to the single parent family, but this should no longer be present in our society.

- **emotional problems**   The parent who has been abandoned by a partner can feel rejected, depressed, lonely and insecure. These feelings can be projected on to the children in the form of neglect or over protectiveness and dependency. However, in many cases the break-up of a relationship may bring relief from tension and quarrelling, and the life of the parent and the children may benefit enormously.

- **other difficulties**   The one-parent family may also have problems with housing, employment, child minding, leisure time activities, loneliness and isolation. Children may feel the effects of being deprived of a mother or father figure, and of living with a single parent who has to bear all the

15

pressures of housework, outside employment and child rearing on her or his own. Usually, it is the way in which these situations are tackled which is important in giving the family an acceptable way of life.

Many single-parent families become **reconstituted families**; that is, the divorced spouses find another partner and remarry.

More than one third of weddings involve remarriage of one or both partners, and almost one in six marriages involve remarriage for both partners.

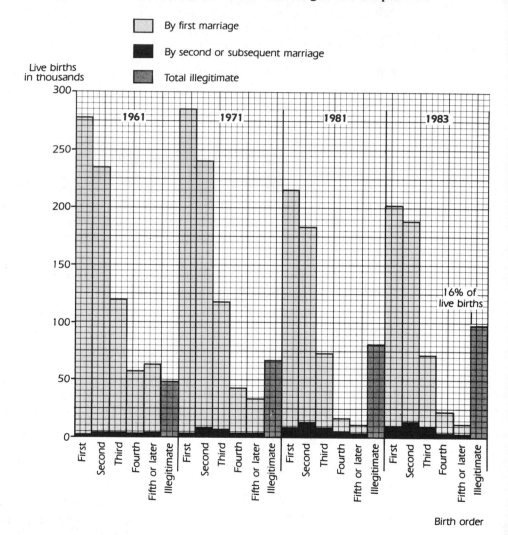

Live births and birth order, 1961–83

Source: *Office of Population Censuses and Surveys*

What does the chart tell you about the number of children born in first marriages compared with second or subsequent marriages?

Is the illegitimacy rate going up or down?

What is the total number of legitimate births for 1983? Is this more or less than in 1961?

What percentage of live births was legitimate in 1983?

The obvious casualties of these second unions may be the children involved. Before they reach the age of 15, one in five children can expect to see their parents divorced. Nine out of ten children under 5 lived with their natural parents in 1985, but this figure drops to seven out of ten for the 15–18 age group.

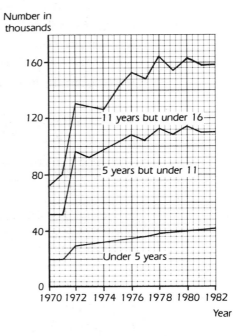

Children under 16 of divorcing couples in England and Wales, 1970–82

Source: *Social Trends 1985*

The Divorce Reform Act (1969) resulted in an increase in the numbers of children affected by divorce. The effects upon the children of marital split-up and having to accept a new mother or father can be very traumatic and give rise to many emotional problems, especially if the children are made to feel that a mother or father does not love them any more and has deserted them. In some cases, however, where there is an amicable family split, the families may become friendly and a new form of extended family may develop.

Although many single- and step-parent families are well adjusted and happy, the facts still remain that they are likely to have the kinds of problem described above, and that more than 50 per cent of children in care in 1984 came from one-parent families.

The changing role of women

These are some of the reasons why a woman with a family may choose to return to work:

- **financial**   The woman's partner may be unemployed or in a low-paid job. She may have a large family or may be a single parent.

- **to improve the standard of living for the family**   Sometimes this might mean a return to work to buy something specific, such as the family's own home, a car or holidays.

- **to make social contacts**   This usually happens when the children start school, and she misses their company.

- **for stimulation**   She may be bored with being at home all day with only young children for company.

- **to achieve a degree of independence**   This might be financial independence, or to get away from the label of being 'just a housewife'.

- **to use the training and skills she acquired earlier**   She may have studied for a professional career such as banking, the law, teaching, nursing, etc.

Approximately 8 million women are in some form of employment, over half of these being married. Many women manage very well to combine a full or part-time job with looking after a home and family, especially if they and their partner work out a pattern of shared work and responsibilities. Problems may arise, however, and these might include:

- difficulties with finding and keeping child minders.
- deciding who is to look after the children during school holidays and before and after school.
- what happens to the children if they are ill.
- the family coming to depend upon the two incomes and perhaps running into financial trouble if the mother suddenly has to stop work.
- parents not being able to agree on how to spend the increased income.
- children having to look after themselves until mother or father returns from work. Safety is a special problem for these 'latch-key children'.
- children possibly feeling deprived of parents' love and attention, leading to emotional problems.
- lack of parental supervision possibly encouraging bad behaviour, such as vandalism, petty thieving, etc.
- the physical stress of doing two full-time jobs being exhausting and leading to physical illnesses.
- the emotional stress leading to family quarrels, family break-up, psychological problems, etc.
- the male partner feeling that he has been ousted as the family provider and resenting his partner's increased independence.

There is an increasing tendency towards role reversal, when the male stays at home to care for the home and family and the female goes out to work. This is especially so if the woman can obtain a better paid job and/or if the man is unemployed or in low-paid employment.

A multicultural society

British society is traditionally very diverse. For centuries it has been made up of groups of people of different ethnic origins. The population of Britain today is made up of groups of people who differ in their religious beliefs, first language and a range of cultural factors from traditional family structure to traditional types of food.

> *What do you consider to be 'traditional' British food? List the main meals you have eaten both at school and at home with your family in the last week. In which countries did the meals originate? How has living in a multicultural society improved and increased our choice of foods?*

It is important to remember that many families who belong to what are sometimes termed 'ethnic minority groups' have lived in Britain for several generations. The total population of Britain in 1985 was 59 235 000. The figures below show the ethnic origin of the people in Britain who make up the ethnic minority groups:

Group	Number in thousands (approx.)
West Indian	547
Indian	689
Pakistani	406
Bangladeshi	99
Chinese	122
African	102
Others	3 423

Source: *Social Trends 1985*

The other 51 222 000 people in Britain make up the ethnic majority of the population.

> *Where do you think the large number of people in the 'Others' group in the table above might have originated from?*

> *The largest numbers of people of West Indian and Guyanese origin live in Greater London, while the largest number of people of Pakistani origin live in the West Midlands and West Yorkshire. Why do you think this is so?*

Living in a multicultural society enriches the lives of all families in that society – they can take part in and enjoy the customs and celebrations of other groups, such as Chinese New Year.

The multicultural society provides a variety of:

- **religions**   Traditionally the majority of people in the UK tended to follow the Christian religion, with a minority following Judaism. With an

19

increasingly multicultural society a wider spread of religions now have followings, such as Hinduism, Islam, Sikhism and so on. What other religions are practised in this country? What are their different festivals? Which ones do you celebrate?

● **language**   Most schools in Britain teach only in English, although in areas where there is a high percentage of people whose first language is not English, specialist teachers may be appointed. In certain parts of Wales, for example, all teaching in a school may be in Welsh. These situations encourage people to be bilingual, which can be a positive advantage.

● **family structure**   Speaking very generally, the traditional Asian family background is close-knit, very much a part of the extended family, and largely male dominated. Many families of ethnic minority groups have lived away from their country of origin for several generations but may still remain part of the 'home-based' extended family in their original country and sometimes return there or send their children there to be educated or to select a partner.

Traditionally Asian women remained at home to look after house and family, and depended upon their female relations for companionship, help and advice. In the traditional Afro-Caribbean family, women have more power than in traditional Asian or Western families, with the family based on mother–child ties rather than father–child or mother–father. In 1984, a third of West Indian households in Britain were headed by women, compared with a quarter of white households and fewer than one in ten Asian households.

40 per cent of Pakistani-origin and Bangladeshi-origin households surveyed in 1985 had four or more dependent children, compared with 4 per cent of West Indian-origin households, 14 per cent of Indian-origin households, and 2 per cent of white households. Can you think of a reason which might explain these figures?

What do you think the words 'prejudice' and 'discrimination' mean? They are often used where one person may be intolerant or have an unfavourable opinion which is based on insufficient evidence, and treats someone from another race or religion unfairly. Anyone, whatever their background, can be guilty of racial prejudice or discrimination. In times when the supply of housing or employment etc. is under pressure, people from ethnic minority groups tend to be the targets of discrimination.

Do you think discrimination is a problem?

What effect do you think it might have on an individual or family which is the target of this sort of discrimination?

In recent years, people of African, Caribbean and some of Asian origin have preferred to be known collectively as 'black'. Why do you think this is so?

Unemployment

The figures in the tables that are shown below indicate the size of the unemployment problem, which exists not only in this country but throughout the world. Unemployment is a complex situation, and the effect upon the family can be drastic. People work for two main reasons: to support themselves and/or their family financially; and because it is a socially acceptable thing to do, and enables them to have the companionship of others at their place of work. The Government, working through the social services, will provide a family or an individual with sufficient money to live, but cannot solve the social problem. This is what causes many family upsets:

- Young people without jobs become bored, resentful and lacking in motivation. They may envy their companions who have satisfactory, well-paid jobs. They may cause trouble at home by being in the way all the time, or they may be tempted into the world of petty crime, drug abuse, alcohol abuse, prostitution, etc.

- The bread winner with a family to support may find that if he or she becomes unemployed the family's standard of living is reduced because of a drastic cut in finance, and there is no money to spare for leisure activities and less necessary items.

  With long-term unemployment he or she may lose job skills, and so become less likely to get another job. Boredom, frustration and lack of money can cause quarrels at home, and he or she may be tempted into petty crime or drinking. He or she loses the companionship of his or her workmates, and the family can become isolated.

Families may become temporarily or permanently split up if the bread winner, in an attempt to find work, moves to another area or into a situation where the family cannot be taken.

Average monthly unemployment figures in the UK

Year	Total in thousands	% rate
1979	1 295.7	5.3
1980	1 664.9	6.8
1981	2 520.4	10.4
1982	2 916.9	12.1
1983	3 104.7	12.9
1984	3 084.5	12.8
1985	3 200.0	13.3
1986	3 210.0	13.3

Comparison with other countries

1986 (Jan.)	% unemployed
Ireland	17.9
Belgium	15.8
UK	13.3
Italy	11.1
France	10.2
America	6.7
Japan	2.8

Young school-leavers

Highly educated people for whom there
are insufficient opportunities

Thirty/forty-year-olds made redundant
because of contracting sales markets

People asked to retire early because of shrinking
numbers of users, or to make financial cuts

What is being done to help people in these groups?

Summary and Evaluation

In this section we have identified the types of family structure in present-day Britain and studied the factors which have brought about the changed situation from Victorian times up to the present day.

Family patterns are constantly being altered by factors such as:

- changing moral values and a greater understanding of family problems.
- world-wide economics which influence our spending power.
- technological and scientific discoveries such as advanced medical research, automation, computers.
- the influence of different ethnic traditions and cultures.
- influence from government and voluntary sources.
- influence from media sources such as TV, radio and newsprint.

There are now wider variations of family structure than in former times. These are not necessarily bad situations – just different. It is often better for children to be in a single-parent family, for example, rather than be constantly subjected to arguments between two parents; an illegitimate child can be just as happy (or happier) being brought up by its natural mother as by foster or adoptive parents; children can learn independence and thought for others if they are in a working mother family; and so on.

Children are resilient and will adapt to a situation, providing they receive a reasonable standard of physical care and love. Family life is adapting to suit changing social circumstances. This does not mean that it is breaking down, but just that families are reacting to present-day values and differing social expectations.

Follow-up Work

Fact finding exercises

1   These are some of the problems which can lead to divorce:

> poor housing conditions
> having no children, though they are wanted
> one partner being away from home for long periods
> living with in-laws
> getting married when very young
> breadwinner being unemployed
> financial insecurity
> one partner having an alcohol problem

Add as many other reasons to this list as you can.

Choose four items from this list and explain why they put a strain upon a marriage.

2   Compare the problems of living in a town with those of living in the country. You could use a table like this:

Living in an urban area	Living in a rural area
1 Pollution of the atmosphere with smoke and fumes	1 Poor shopping facilities
2 Traffic congestion	2 Inadequate public transport

3   These factors have been suggested as reasons why women live longer than men:

> men have a lot of stress and pressure at work
>
> women are physically safer working at home than men working in industry
>
> the tendency is for men to lose interest in life after they retire from their work
>
> men have more stress because they have more financial responsibilities.

Now that a high proportion of women also take employment outside the home, do you think that this gap will be narrowed? Give reasons.

4 Explain the meaning of the following terms:

role-reversal infant mortality rate
birth rate new town
death rate lone-parent family
urbanisation reconstituted family
rural community recession

Data response and problem solving exercises

1 Better standards of hygiene and health care have increased life expectancy in the UK. Look at the graph, and answer the questions that follow.

a) What was the average life expectancy in 1850?

b) What was the average life expectancy in 1981 (male and female)?

c) How do you think the increase in life expectancy has affected family structures? How do you think it is likely to affect them in future?

Life expectancy in the UK, 1850–1981

Source: *Government Actuary's Department*

2 Jane has a full-time job, five days a week. Tim, her husband, is temporarily unemployed. They have a five-year old son, Luke, who attends the infant school. Tim is studying at home to improve his job prospects. Jane enjoys cooking. They have a small bungalow, an old car and the usual labour-saving equipment.

a) How much of the housework should be done by Tim? Give reasons.

b) Allocate the household chores between Jane and Tim and plan the weekly routine.

c) Plan a typical weekday routine for Tim.

d) Suggest four leisure-time activities which could involve the whole family.

e) If they had an unexpected windfall of £250, would you suggest they spent it on a deepfreeze or a microwave cooker? Give reasons.

3 Jas, whose family comes from India, has a girlfriend, Julie, who is white. Jas and Julie are considering marriage. They both know that their parents will be against the idea and they realise the problems which a mixed marriage may bring.

a) List some of the possible problems of a mixed marriage.

b) Where, and to whom, could Julie and Jas go to get advice?

c) What is the best way to approach both sets of parents to explain the situation?

4 Chloe and John have three young children. John has a good job but he works long hours and is often tired and under stress. He goes to the pub two or three times a week and plays football at the weekends. Chloe is bored and lonely and has few friends, and they live a long way from family and relations. The couple are constantly quarrelling and are considering separation.

These are some of the steps they could take:

John could try to get another job, nearer to his or his wife's family.

They could employ a mother's help and Chloe could try to get a part-time job.

Chloe could join a Mother and Toddler group, Meet-a-Mum Association, Housewives' League or church group.

They could employ a baby-sitter and both join a leisure club, theatre group, dramatic society or social club.

They could seek the advice of the Marriage Guidance Council.

They could decide to have a 'trial separation' for three months to see how they managed apart.

They could make amicable plans for separation, with John continuing to support his family financially. This would end the stress imposed on themselves and the children by their constant bickering.

a) State the advantages for each of these courses of action.

b) Write a paragraph about three of these courses, describing how the family got along after taking and putting into practice each of these decisions.

c) Describe ways which could have helped to avoid this situation developing in the first place.

Free response questions

1   Describe the advantages and disadvantages of belonging to a nuclear family.

2   What influence have the Divorce Reform Act (1969) and the Abortion Act (1967) had on the family? The divorce rates chart on p. 9 and the number of abortions chart on p. 10 should help you.

3   In many instances, people from different ethnic groups integrate to form a community. In some instances, relations between the different groups could be improved. Suggest how – consider housing, language, education, finance, etc.

Activities

1   Carry out a survey of the amenities in your area for parents with young children.

Question a cross-section of parents if possible, including those in a poor/medium/good financial situation; those in a good/deprived area; different social classes; and employed and unemployed.

Put together a booklet or fact sheet which could be of use to families with young children who live in your area, which could cover:

    organisations for parents and young children

    local health centres and clinics

    baby-sitting groups

    local transport

    local shopping facilities, including markets and shops selling second-hand equipment

    parks, swimming pools and other recreational facilities

    state and private schools in your area

    a list of child-minders and day nurseries

2   Parents with young children need:

    social contact with other parents

    play-group facilities

    good shopping facilities

    baby sitters

    expert advice on childhood problems

    good educational facilities

    good public transport

Put this list in order of importance. Add points of your own to the list.

How can parents help *themselves* to get these things?

3   *Woman's Hour* on Radio 4 is a very popular programme and covers an extensive range of topics. As quite a lot of men are at home during this time (2 p.m.–3 p.m.) how could you:

    a)   adapt the programme to suit women *and* men? Suggest a suitable title.

    b)   plan a programme called *Men's Hour*? Suggest the contents.

Which of the above plans would you favour and why?

In fact, many men already listen to the programme. Why do you think this is?

SECTION B The Family Background

3 Functions of the Family

The family unit exists within this country in many varied and changing forms, but the main functions of the family have remained largely the same. They are:

- in the first place, to have children and to establish a lasting relationship.

- secondly, to nurture the children of the relationship; to care for the needs of the weaker members of the family, i.e. the young, old, sick and handicapped; and to play a *supportive* role to all the individual members of the family.

- thirdly for *socialisation*; that is, to teach the children the cultural and traditional background of the society in which they live and to help them to play their part accepting from, and giving to, this society.

In Britain, these family functions are traditionally carried out against a background of married life, where a man or woman selects and marries one partner (**monogamy**) and they live together for the rest of their lives. Their children live with them until they leave to set up homes of their own. Three quarters of the world's population live in communities where monogamy is practised, but in some cultures traditions are different. They may allow a man to have more than one wife (**polygyny**), as Moslem and some Mormon groups do; or they may allow a woman to have more than one husband (**polyandry**), as in parts of Tibet. The general term for both these practices is **polygamy**.

The responsibilities taken by each member of the family also vary widely. If the man is dominant, and usually the head of the household, this is a **patriarchal** society. If the woman is the head of the family, this is a **matriarchal** society. In some cultures it is a child's parents who select a suitable marriage partner for him or her. In India, Afghanistan and other Moslem and Hindu countries, these **arranged marriages** are the normal practice.

Traditionally, in the West, the family is an individual unit, but in some parts of the world **communal living** takes place. This means a couple may marry or live together and produce children, but the child rearing and some aspects of family life are in part taken over by the community or the State. In the **kibbutz** system, which occurs in Israel, all the infants are separated from their parents and reared in Children's Houses, only seeing their parents for a short time each day. The system is not so rigid these days, and the separation between parents and children is less complete, with some children spending the night with their parents. In Communist China, groups are formed called **communes**. Children are looked after from an early age at the communal crèches and nurseries, and much of the responsibility of child rearing is taken from the parents, who are then expected to work for the good of the commune.

These varieties of family life have all evolved to suit the needs and beliefs of the people of different cultures.

Perhaps some of the members of your group have experience of these situations. Have a general discussion and try to discover the advantages of:

having a marriage partner chosen for you by your parents.

having more than one husband or wife.

having a man or woman as the undisputed head of the family.

living in a kibbutz.

Family relationships

It is generally accepted that children happily develop into well-adjusted, secure adults, able to give and accept loving relationships, if they come from a settled, supportive and disciplined home background. A high proportion of children are cared for by one or more of their natural parents, often having close contact with grandparents and other family relations. In these circumstances the child can more easily identify with his or her family background and have a feeling of belonging.

Parents

It is not an easy job to be a parent. Parents have a much greater influence upon their children than probably any other factor. Although the influence of schools and friends is important, parents must accept the responsibility for bringing up a child to be well adjusted and acceptable to other people. Basically a boy is likely to be more influenced by the attitudes and activities of his father, and a girl to learn from the behaviour of her mother. Children will take their standards from the examples set by their parents or parent substitute.

Parents are influenced in the way they bring up their children by many factors:

- **their own childhood and the way they were treated** A person with a happy, secure childhood will usually make a success of dealing with his or her own children. Adults who have themselves been ill-treated or neglected as children are more likely to treat their own children in the same way, but sometimes they do the reverse and overprotect or spoil them.

- **the influence of grandparents and relatives** Sometimes parents have themselves got very dominant mothers or fathers who are determined to see their grandchildren brought up in the way they think best. If parents are very young, unsure of themselves or easily led, they may be unable to overcome the interference of well meaning relatives.

- **traditional cultural values** Some parents bring up their children in a traditional way, trying to maintain the culture they grew up in themselves. This may mean they expect the children to live in the same areas as father or mother, go to the same schools, aim for the same occupations, believe in the same things, and follow the same way of life. This can restrict the individual child, and if there is a difference between the behaviour expected at home and the behaviour expected at school, the children may develop dual standards. It also, however, keeps up the wide and developing range of cultures within UK society.

- **the expectations of the community in which they live**   Society exerts tremendous pressures upon the way in which we all live and many parents conform to the pattern of those living around them.

- **their own personality traits**   If they are quiet, thoughtful introverted people they will tend to produce children who are the same; noisy, extrovert parents often have children with the same characteristics.

- **the media**   Programmes on television, stories and articles in magazines, and advertising, can often give a very distorted picture of family life. Parents may think that they should try to be the same as the glossy pictures show, and they may strive for unrealistic standards shown by the media.

- **practical factors**   Things such as family income, housing conditions, working conditions, and state of health, can contribute to the way in which parents treat their children.

There are many types of family, who may all be happy in their own individual ways.

Parents need to have a lot of different qualities to be able to bring up a family. Which of those shown below do you think are the most important to be?

even-tempered	*conscientious*	*cheerful*	*sympathetic*
fair	*hard working*	*generous*	*self-denying*
imaginative	*creative*	*strict*	*easy-going*
affectionate	*adventurous*	*self-controlled*	

Which of these qualities do you think you have got?

Ask a friend to make a list of the qualities which he or she thinks you have got.

Would you make a good parent?

Which qualities will you need to develop to make you a good parent?

Why do many very young people have difficulty with the responsibilities of parenthood?

The relationship between parent and child is very close and complex. For his first few years a child is totally dependent upon his parents (or carers) for his physical and emotional needs. Gradually he must be allowed to become independent, whilst still retaining the security of the close family bond. This can be a difficult process: some parents are unable to release their children, some children are too insecure to accept independence. The rebellious teenager may be the result of an over-restricted childhood; the clinging, insecure teenager may be the result of a lack of opportunities to be independent.

Siblings (brothers and sisters)

The relationship between brothers and sisters is a very special one and differs from that between other relations and in peer groups. Parents worry that their children argue, fight, are jealous and spiteful to each other, but these are perfectly natural reactions. Arguments can be healthy, and repressed feelings can be dangerous. If you have a brother or sister, you probably know that you can have a fiery quarrel and say nasty things to each other, and make it up a few hours later. You can even enjoy the luxury of having feelings of hate for them because they will be quickly replaced by feelings of love.

Parents must try to:

- establish a secure background for all their children.
- have a system of fairness for all.
- give the same amount of love and attention to all.
- include all the children in family activities.
- help to sort out disagreements, while letting the children sort it out for themselves as much as possible.
- discourage bullying, tale-telling, jealousy and selfishness, and encourage generosity, helpfulness, protectiveness and affection.
- where a child needs special care, as in the case of a handicapped or ill child, encourage the help and involvement of the others.
- regard each child as an individual with his own belongings, interests and personality.
- avoid being over-possessive or over-protective towards any one child. This may happen with the youngest child especially.

The position of the child in the family structure will have an important influence on behaviour and character.

The first-born child

These children are often very much wanted and planned for. They usually receive the complete love and care of their parents for at least the first year of their lives, and they are encouraged by their parents to develop quickly. First-born children often develop powers of leadership, and many prominent and successful people in our society were first-born children.

Advantages	Disadvantages
They receive the undivided attention of parents and other relations.	They may be over-protected and indulged.
They are encouraged to achieve physical and intellectual milestones quickly.	Too much attention may be focused on them.
Their achievements are noted and rewarded.	Too much may be expected of them, and they may be stretched beyond their capabilities.
It is easier to cope financially with the first child, who will benefit materially.	They may be given too much responsibility.
They are given responsibility and independence when the other children of the family are born.	If they have been given a lot of attention, they may find it difficult to cope with the idea of a new baby in the family.
	Parents are still experimenting with ideas of child rearing.

The middle child

These children may feel more secure, as they have the love and attention of their parents, and a brother or sister as well. Sometimes they may be aggressive because they feel they have to fight for some of the attention which is being given to the eldest or the youngest.

Advantages	Disadvantages
They feel security within a family.	They may feel inadequate if compared with older children in the family.
They have the companionship of an older brother or sister.	They may be bullied by an older sibling who feels jealous or left out.
They have care and encouragement from other siblings.	They may not get so many material possessions, and may have to have the older child's cast-offs.
They do not have to go into 'unknown territory'.	They could feel left out if attention is lavished on older or younger siblings.

They can take sides, and get support from siblings in arguments with parents and outsiders.

Parents have more experience and may have more relaxed attitudes.

Their development may be retarded because the older child does everything for them.

They may be pushed too hard to compete with the elder sibling.

The youngest child

These children often arrive as a member of an established family. They are the babies of the family, and may be spoilt and pampered. They often remain good-tempered and well adjusted but can be very demanding and expect to have it all their own way.

Advantages

They are usually given a lot of love and attention.

They feel secure and have the companionship of older siblings

They have plenty of close family support when needed.

Older children may help with the learning processes.

Parents have a lot of experience of how to deal with childhood problems, and how to get the best health care, education, etc.

Disadvantages

They may suffer some neglect because of lack of money.

They may be over-indulged and treated as a pet.

Parents may not have planned for them and they may be unwanted.

Parents may be fairly old for child rearing and have less time and energy.

Older children may resent having to look after the younger children.

The only child

It is easy for only children to become spoilt because of doting parents. Their parents must aim not to give in to their every whim, but allow them to develop their own personalities, fight their own battles and discipline them when they do wrong. These children must be trained to be independent and allowed to mix socially with other children at as early an age as possible.

Advantages

They will probably get a lot of love and attention from their parents.

They do not have to share their parents' attention with other siblings.

They may benefit from having more material possessions.

Their parents may have more time to sit and teach and encourage them, so aiding their development.

Disadvantages

They may miss out on the companionship of other siblings.

They could have difficulty making outside relationships.

Parents may be over-protective and over-indulgent, so making these children timid, unadventurous, selfish and demanding.

The large family

In the nineteenth century, the average British family had five or six children, and some families had ten or more. Many of today's families have two or three children.

What is it like to be one of a large family?

Advantages	**Disadvantages**
The children are part of a large, close family unit.	The children may feel neglected and overlooked.
They always have someone to take their side in arguments.	There will be a lack of privacy and of space for homework, hobbies, etc.
They have the opportunity to develop independently and assume early responsibilities.	The family may suffer financial deprivation and housing problems.
They have plenty of companionship and things to do.	Older children may be given too much responsibility for the care of young ones.
They have the chance of adventure and exploration within a secure family framework.	Each child may get insufficient time and attention from parents.
They are not constantly over-shadowed or influenced by parents.	Bad behaviour may be overlooked, or discipline may be too harsh.

Twins and triplets

These are often looked upon with envy by other children because they feel that twins and triplets always have someone to play with, always have support, and never have to face a new situation alone. Twins and triplets do enjoy these benefits and identical twins (*uniovular*) have a very close relationship throughout their lives. Fraternal twins (*binovular*) act like ordinary brothers or sisters. It can be very difficult for twins to develop their own personalities, especially if parents insist upon dressing and treating them exactly the same. They are often referred to as 'the twins', rather than by name, and thus become very dependent upon each other. The parents' or carers' love and attention has to be shared right from the start of life, and money and possessions have to be shared too. Language development may be retarded because the twins develop their own sign language or thought patterns.

All these factors may restrict their contact with others and may lead to friction or emotional problems later in life. Parents of twins should try to make sure that the twins mix with other children, and are not allowed to become overdependent upon each other. They should be treated as separate individuals, and given separate loving. Other children in the family should not be made to feel neglected or excluded.

Schools and other organisations should be made aware of the parents' views. Useful help and information may be obtained from the Twins' Clubs Association.

The handicapped child
Handicapped children can affect the life of the family very much, bringing difficulties and benefits. These factors are dealt with in Section C.

Sibling problems

It is very common for siblings to argue and fight amongst themselves, but sometimes these feelings become deep seated, and specific problems arise which should be dealt with quickly. Sometimes professional help is required.

Jealousy
This is a very common problem and usually occurs when an older child feels pushed out by the arrival of a new baby. Children are naturally egocentric (self-centred) and resent it when their importance is diminished. Even when the child is prepared for the new baby's arrival it can still be a shock and he can show his jealousy in many ways:

- becoming very demanding and attention-seeking.
- displaying antisocial behaviour, becoming noisy and aggressive, having temper tantrums.
- developing nervous habits such as nail biting, hair chewing, bed wetting, and twitches.
- becoming withdrawn, moody, quiet and miserable.
- taking it out on the baby by pinching, biting or slapping when he is pretending to play with the child.
- deliberately breaking the baby's toys and damaging the child's possessions.

The pre-school child will show his jealousy fiercely and openly. The older child may try to control and repress his feelings, but they may emerge at a later stage and cause a rift in the family.

Sensible parents will deal with jealousy patiently but firmly, as follows:
- Prepare the child well in advance for the birth of a new baby. Allow him to join in with the preparations, but do not overdo the fuss.
- Do not be disappointed if the child is not especially thrilled with the new arrival.
- Always try to involve him when feeding, bathing and playing with the new baby. Both parents and grandparents can play an important part in seeing that he does not feel neglected.
- Show patience and understanding with bed wetting, telling lies, temper tantrums, etc.
- Give him lots of praise and small rewards when he does things well. (Do *not* try to make up for lack of attention by giving him expensive presents and letting him have all his own way.)

- Distract him when he is being troublesome and give him something else to do.

- Give him plenty to do generally. Make him feel important, and try to give him new interests outside the home such as joining a mother and toddler group.

- In the case of an older child, discuss the situation with him and let him see that you understand his feelings of rejection, but that parents can have enough love for everyone.

- Inform the child's school so that they can deal sympathetically with behaviour and learning difficulties.

Sibling rivalry

Competitiveness between siblings is always there to some degree and can last for a lifetime. The children in a family feel that they are competing with each other for their parents' love and attention. The youngest one may resent his older siblings being bigger, stronger, better-looking or cleverer. Competition is not always a bad thing and may lead to a child's working harder to try to catch up with a brother or sister and capture parents' approval. Constant failure no matter how much he tries, however, can result in a sullen refusal to try again, and lead to behavioural problems.

Parents must be aware of this natural rivalry and never show favouritism towards any one child, or be over critical with another. A child who is constantly being unfavourably compared with his siblings will feel insecure and unhappy and can develop severe emotional problems. Parents can see that jobs around the house are shared out equally, each child having his own responsibility and being praised and rewarded for it. Having brothers and sisters can teach a child how to share and be generous, yet still retain his own individuality.

The ill-treated child

Unhappily in some families there may be one child who is unwanted and rejected. The child may be weaker than the others, he may have a handicap or he may not have been wanted by his parents from the first. The siblings may follow the example of the parents and pick on the one child to bully, torment and isolate from family activities. It is not unusual to find a child who is treated in this way in an otherwise happy and normal family, and there have been extreme cases of a rejected child kept isolated in a bedroom or outhouse.

These cases are difficult to identify, and teachers, social workers, playgroup leaders, etc. should watch for signs which could indicate an ill-treated, rejected child from an apparently normal home background (see pp. 58–9).

Aggressiveness

This is a characteristic which can be damaging or, if kept under control, an asset in later life if a forceful personality is needed for certain jobs.

The aggressive child may come from aggressive parents or have siblings who bully or ridicule him. He may have been made to feel inadequate and therefore tries to relieve his feelings on others who are weaker than he is. At playgroup you will see the child who charges round, knocking other children over, snatching their toys, breaking things, and causing trouble. This child is an unhappy one, crying out for love and attention. It is probable that he is neglected or bullied, over- or under-disciplined at home. The jealousy he feels for his brothers or sisters may have turned into aggression towards others.

He should not be smacked, shouted at or severely punished. He needs patience, firmness, a clear routine, attention, affection, and plenty of praise when he does anything well.

Severely disturbed children will need psychiatric help.

The withdrawn child

It is quite common to see a solitary child playing or working on his own in the playground, at playgroup or in the park. Some children are naturally quiet and reserved and enjoy spells of playing by themselves. There is a difference between this type of child and the child who is withdrawn and frightened because of bullying and ill-treatment.

Severe withdrawal symptoms occur when a child cannot cope with the external stresses put upon him. These may be: bullying from parents and siblings; feelings of insecurity when parents do not want him, or if they separate; trauma caused by the death of someone close to him; over-anxious parents; or parents who are expecting too much from him. The child will withdraw into his own world, living in imaginary surroundings and talking to imaginary playmates. A seriously withdrawn child will require skilled psychiatric treatment.

Every child passes through difficult stages; it is a natural part of growing up. Parents who are sensitive to the needs of their children will be able to sort out family problems before they do very much damage.

Grandparents

The relationship between children and grandparents can be a very rewarding one. It should benefit parents, children and grandparents. Many grandparents are young in age and/or outlook. They have their own jobs and interests but will still find time to love and care for their grandchildren. Parents should make sure that the relationship between their family and their own parents is a close one and as free from friction as possible.

Parents can set a good example to their own children by the way they care for their ageing parents. If they show love and concern, their children will grow up knowing that this is the correct attitude. If children are encouraged to ridicule or defy their grandparents, how will they act when their own parents become elderly? Children should be taught that as their grandparents get older they will become less active; they may develop physical or mental problems; they will need to rest more and may become irritable and less tolerant. The child can then be taught to show understanding and compassion.

These are some ways in which grandparents can enrich family life:

- provide a relaxed and welcoming atmosphere for the family.
- be there for the children to confide in, to discuss problems with, to plan little surprises for mum and dad with.
- provide an opportunity for escape from the pressures of home life. If there has been a family quarrel or the child is feeling miserable, grandparents can be good listeners.
- look after the children to give their parents a break, by babysitting while they shop, go out for the evening or take a short holiday.
- act as a buffer if parents separate or divorce. They can provide some continuity and security until the situation settles down.
- act as a mother/father substitute in single-parent families or if both parents are at work.
- take the grandchildren on outings to the seaside, to the park, to visit other relations, to the pantomime, etc. It is an opportunity for the children to get a little spoiling, which does not hurt once in a while.
- have the time and patience to pass on skills and interests, such as fishing, embroidery, bird watching, gardening and storytelling.
- show concern at failure, give praise and reward for achievement and gentle reproach for bad behaviour, and help to mend family arguments.
- help to pass on family traditions, passing on tales relating to past experiences of family members – including mum and/or dad.
- care for the grandchildren while mother is having another baby or if there is family illness.

Some grandparents are not very co-operative. They feel they have got to interfere and try to impose their ways and standards. Perhaps they do not like their child's partner and are always critical of their efforts at parenting. Friction can sometimes arise when a grandparent has to live with the family and he or she objects to noise and untidiness, or to the child's friends, schoolwork, activities, manners and general progress.

It is a difficult situation and parents must make it plain that they will bring up their children in their own way. Grandparents should try to:

- give advice only when it is asked for.
- keep out of the way sometimes and give parents and children time to themselves.

- avoid troublesome situations.
- realise that their ways and standards may be outdated and inappropriate for modern-day life.

A child's life should be extended to include elderly people, and if there are no natural grandparents other elderly relatives or neighbours should be drawn into the family circle, or perhaps a lonely old person could be befriended.

> *Discuss the value of your grandparents in your life. If you have no grandparents, do you feel the lack of them?*
>
> *Has your attitude to elderly people been influenced by your relationship with your grandparents?*
>
> *How do you feel when you read about atrocities to frail old people by young thugs?*

Other family relations

Maintaining contact with other family relations can give a child a valuable sense of belonging and a feeling of security. A child who has several cousins, aunts and uncles has a life which extends beyond his own immediate family. If he has no brothers or sisters he can turn to his cousins for companionship.

Many families now move away from their original environment and it is easy to lose contact with family relations. Parents should try to maintain contact by:

- visiting as often as possible and welcoming them for visits.
- telephoning or writing to exchange family news.
- asking for advice and discussing future plans with them.
- taking cousins on holiday or on outings.
- attending family occasions such as christenings, birthday parties, weddings and funerals.
- sending cards and presents at birthdays, Christmas, etc.
- making it clear that they will always try to give help and support in case of difficulty.

Socialisation

The child who has the security of a happy family background is very fortunate, but he must also learn how to get along with other people, because eventually he is going to have to meet, make friends and live with people outside his immediate family circle. If he has an established place within his own family, he will have the confidence to make social contact with others.

Socialisation begins at a very early stage and social contacts are first made by parents. Parents who are warm friendly people and make friends easily often pass this on to their children. Children who are not allowed to mix or who are not taught to be aware of other people can become selfish and introverted and may develop antisocial attitudes in later life.

43

Social development and the stages of socialisation are dealt with more fully in Volume 1, but the chart below shows the basic stages:

Stage	Development
1 *The first year*	*The child enjoys the company of his parents, siblings and close family.*
	He is still anxious and shy with strangers.
	He needs close physical and emotional contact with one person.
2 *1–2 years*	*He is acquiring social skills such as helping to feed and dress himself and learning the beginnings of speech.*
	His personality is developing and he may be happy to be left with a familiar figure for a few hours.
3 *2–3 years*	*He is becoming a sociable being and enjoys playing alongside other children.*
	He is becoming less dependent upon his parents.
4 *3–5 years*	*The acquisition of speech helps him to develop social contact.*
	He likes to play with other children and shows affection for others.
	He is becoming increasingly independent.
5 *5–12 years*	*He may have a best friend or be one of a gang.*
	He begins to question his parents' attitudes and authority.
	He should by this stage be well adjusted, sociable and reasonably independent.

To enable a child to develop socially and achieve independence parents should try to:

- provide a stable home background.
- set aside some time during the day to give attention to the child.
- encourage contact with other people as the child becomes ready for it.
- mix with others outside the family circle by: joining clubs; visiting parks, leisure centres, swimming pools; becoming involved with team games; joining the PTA, etc.
- encouraging the child to bring friends home or visit his friends' houses.
- get the child used to being left with other adults for a few hours, in preparation for when he starts school.
- give him the experience of a playgroup or nursery school.
- not over-protect the child nor encourage clinging, grizzling or tale-telling.
- be pleased when the child is brave when going to the dentist, or if he has a bump, a disappointment, etc.
- teach the child basic social skills, such as good table manners, toilet training, points of hygiene, etc., so that he does not feel embarrassed or out of place with other people.

- not interfere in children's squabbles.
- recognise that children need to be alone sometimes.
- teach the child that if he wants to be popular and keep his friends, he must be pleasant and considerate to other people.

The clinging, shy child
Most children pass through a clinging stage, and most children are shy when meeting new people or in new situations. Parents may worry because they feel their child is lonely and without friends. It should be made clear that this is a normal condition and the child should be helped to overcome his shyness. Parents can help by:

- not forcing the pace. Allow the child to face the situation in his own time and in his own way.
- not constantly drawing attention to the child's shyness or showing anxiety at his lack of social success.
- giving the child the support of having a familiar figure with him when he meets new acquaintances or situations.
- inviting children home to play – the child will feel more secure at home.
- giving gentle, sympathetic encouragement, never bullying or poking fun.
- letting the child realise that if he is busy thinking about other people he will not have time to think about his own shyness.
- realising that a clinging, shy child is often insecure. Try to build up his self-confidence and make him feel loved and wanted.

It is part of the process of growing up for young people to want to help others. They should be encouraged to:

- have consideration for their friends.
- be helpful to the neighbours.
- join in community help schemes.
- help with school functions.
- help those who are worse off than themselves, e.g. the handicapped, the housebound.

This will help them to mix and to become a part of the community.

Responsibilities of parenthood

Parenting is a very demanding job and the results of failure can be very severe. We often blame parents and the family background when a child grows up to be antisocial, badly behaved and emotionally mixed up. Parents usually feel guilty when their children behave badly and wonder where they themselves have gone wrong; yet modern families are usually child centred, with the children as the most important members of the household. Parents have more time for their children as the average working week becomes shorter and the average family size becomes smaller.

Some sociologists believe that children are being given too much attention, too much freedom and too many material possessions, but too few challenging situations where they need to show initiative, perseverence and a sense of responsibility. This leads to boredom and may develop into antisocial behaviour such as football hooliganism, vandalism, petty thieving and aggression. A bored youngster with no opportunities for excitement and adventure can turn to illegal drugs, glue sniffing, alcohol or smoking just for the thrill of it and to flout authority.

Some of the aims of parents should be to:

- provide opportunities for physical, emotional and intellectual development and to give stimulation in the form of toys, games, books, outings, discussions, etc.

- provide a satisfactory model for children to base themselves upon.

- recognise and develop artistic and imaginative qualities and give opportunities for drawing, painting, music, dancing, craft work, etc., so encouraging creative skills.

- give the time required for a child to discuss any problems he may have, noting signs of anxiety, and discuss matters relating to sex education, sexual relationships, death, and how to deal with strong feelings such as jealousy, hatred, etc.

- teach the difference between right and wrong, and what is expected from him.

- give guidance and show disapproval when he misbehaves, but always provide a caring background whatever his misdeeds.

- give information upon moral and spiritual beliefs.

- maintain their own cultural traditions while teaching the child how to fit into a changing community.

- encourage racial harmony.

- train the child to be independent and socially acceptable.

- maintain family contact.

- teach the child how to control but not suppress his emotions.

A child's parents may come from very different backgrounds and they may have very different ideas about bringing up children, but they must try to pull together, discuss each situation and be prepared to compromise.

Parental roles

The charts that follow give a very broad view of traditional parental roles in British society, and of modern developments in these roles.

Traditional roles

Mother	Father
• Home-based to do household tasks – cooking, cleaning, shopping, laundry, menu planning	• Head of the household
• Household spending and accounts	• Breadwinner – going out to work
• Caring for the physical needs of the children	• Disciplining the children
• Teaching social skills	• Money management
• Care during family illness	• Decision making in family affairs
• Looking after aged parents and relations	• Responsible for renting/buying and choosing the family home
• Social contact with family and neighbours	• Planning for holidays and family treats
• Liaison with children's schools	• Interested in affairs outside the home – politics, sport, his own friends
• Choosing items for the home	• Working long hours, little time for his family
• Buying clothing	
• In poorer households, supplementing family income, usually through unskilled work	

Modern developments

Mother	Father
• Running a home and a full-time job	• May choose not to work, or be unemployed, and care for the children while the mother goes to work
• Sharing the children's upbringing with her partner	• Sharing child rearing with mother
• Sharing financial matters	• Sharing the disciplining and policy making with partner
• May have better paid, higher status job than partner	• Taking an active interest in menu planning and cooking; sharing equally in shopping and choosing household appliances
• Discussing all family matters with partner and sharing equally in making decisions	• Planning leisure-time activities with partner
• May be head of a single-parent family	• Sharing financial control and decisions
	• May work full time and care for home and family as a single father

Some families are still run on a very traditional basis, where the male/female roles are clearly defined. In most families today the mother/father roles are more interchangeable than in the past, and the rigid family life-style has been replaced with more relaxed attitudes, parents being of equal status and sharing parental responsibilities.

The basic responsibilities of parents are to meet the child's needs. These are:

physical: for food, warmth, shelter, clothing; and

emotional: for love, security, companionship, discipline.

The present-day family is subjected to many pressures and problems which can cause stress and anxiety and, in extreme cases, marital breakdown. These pressures include:

- unemployment.
- a society in which material possessions are very important.
- social attitudes which do not regard mothering as important work.
- a decline in spiritual values and guidance from religious beliefs.
- increased vandalism, violence and crime among young offenders.

- a generally accepted idea that parental discipline is old-fashioned.
- a changing education system which parents may find difficult to understand.
- the increasing use and ease of obtaining illegal drugs and alcohol.
- the influence of sexually explicit and violent films, videos and the written and spoken word on the developing minds of young people.
- the pressures of advertising to make us spend money on things we do not need and cannot afford.

Parents must be very strong willed to resist these pressures without appearing to be 'spoilsports'.

Split into two groups, for and against, to debate the motion:

   This country would be a better place for young people to grow up in if we returned to traditional family life-styles.

4 Families in Trouble with the Law

Our modern way of life is often described as living in a permissive society. Some adults gloomily believe that law and order are breaking down and that 'it was never like this when we were young'. Those who put together and present the news encourage these ideas because scenes of violence, such as football hooligans, race riots, and vandalism, are given prominence on our TV screens; and newspapers tend to report the more sensational cases of crime, such as robbery with violence, rape, drug abuse, and attacks on old people, which they know will interest their readers.

Crime statistics

The statistics that follow show that crime is increasing.

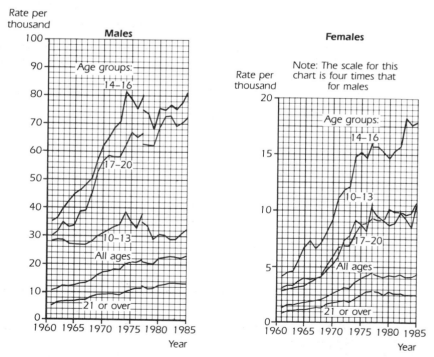

Offenders found guilty of, or cautioned for, indictable offences in England and Wales, 1961–1985

Source: *Social Trends 17, 1987*

(After 1976, the method of recording these statistics changed slightly.)

Crime is increasing especially amongst young people, but the majority of people are law abiding and criminals are a very small minority.

N.B. An **indictable offence** is one which is usually tried before judge and jury. A **non-indictable offence** is less serious and tried in a magistrates' court. A **notifiable offence** is an indictable offence, or any type of criminal damage.

A **caution** is a formal warning to an offender; it is an alternative to prosecution but is not given unless the person admits the offence.

Young offenders, i.e. those over 10 and under 17, are dealt with in special juvenile courts. These courts are held in private and the aim is to reform and help as well as to punish.

The minimum age for prosecution is 10. Children younger than this are dealt with by social casework or care proceedings.

Further facts

In England and Wales:

- there were 3 000 000 notifiable offences in 1984 – an increase of 8 per cent on the previous year.
- boys and young men are responsible for most of the crimes committed: over half the men committing crimes are under 21.
- the highest rate of conviction or caution for indictable offences per thousand of population between 1961 and 1984 was for boys aged 14–16.
- the number of children aged from 10 to 13 convicted of indictable offences in 1984 was 64 000. The number of children aged from 14 to 16 convicted of indictable offences in 1984 was 140 300.
- juvenile crimes of violence more than trebled from 1969 to 1983. They increased from 3624 (1969) to 12 435 (1983).
- the most common crimes are stealing and vandalising cars, vans and motor bikes, or stealing from them.
- nearly 1 : 3 men have been convicted of an offence (excluding motoring offences) by the age of 28.
- over two thirds of young offenders put into custody return to the courts within two years of discharge.
- in 1983, 86 per cent of the 124 000 people who were cautioned were under 17 years old.

Which age group has the greatest number of offenders? (See graphs on p. 50.)

By how many male offenders did the 17–20 age group rise between 1961 and 1984?

Do these charts suggest that females are more law abiding than males?

By how many female offenders did the 14–16 age group rise between 1961 and 1984?

Examples of notifiable offences recorded by the police in England and Wales, in thousands

	1981	**1983**	**1985**
Violence against the person	100.2	111.3	121.7
Sexual offences	19.4	20.4	21.5
Theft and handling stolen goods	1603.2	1705.9	1884.1
Criminal damage	386.7	443.3	539.0

Other types of offences also show a general upward trend in numbers.

Prison population in the UK, 1884 and 1984

	1884	**1984**
UK population	35 962 000	56 488 000
Prison population	28 000 (0.078 %)	48 000 (0.085 %)

Proportionately this is only a small increase, although the UK has generally had a quite high proportion of prisoners compared with other European countries.

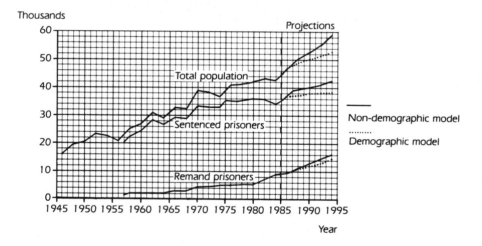

Average population of prison establishments in England and Wales: actuals and projections, 1946–94

Source: *Social Trends 1986*

By how many thousands did the total prison population increase between 1946 and 1985?

By how many thousands is it expected to increase between 1985 and 1993?

The number of police in Britain increased from 39 000 in 1884 to 135 000 in 1984. This is a present-day ratio of 1 member of the police : 400 of the population.

Dealing with crime

The rise in crime figures is very disturbing, and the government is constantly trying to find better ways of reducing them. These include:

- trying to prevent crime before it happens. Methods include establishing crime prevention squads to give advice to householders and business firms; introducing 'hit trains' to help spot bands of juvenile railway vandals; placing TV cameras at sports grounds to spot the trouble makers, etc.

- increasing and improving the police force by giving them better training and updating police procedures.

- introducing community police, i.e. police on the beat who know the local people and can deal with local problems.

- liaising with the leaders of community groups to encourage co-operation.

- encouraging people to help themselves, by becoming involved in Neighbourhood Watch schemes and being security conscious.

- establishing an educational programme. This is done by using TV, radio and pamphlets on crime prevention, drug misuse, drink-driving campaigns, etc.; and sending police representatives to schools and organisations to give talks and demonstrations on security, personal self-defence, child abuse, etc.

Reasons why crimes are committed

We must also study the reasons why people break the law, especially juveniles, as this is where the biggest increase in crime is shown.

Some reasons include:

- **boredom**, especially amongst young people who are unemployed or in employment which is unsatisfying. They may turn to crime as a source of excitement, for the thrill of 'getting away with it', or to show off to their friends.

- **greed**   People who envy other people their possessions and are too lazy to work for what they want may turn to crime.

- **wanting to make a gesture against society**   Vandalism is often a sign of rebellion in young people.

- **parents who have abandoned their responsibilities** for training their children to fit into society.

- **parents who actively set a bad example** by being involved in crime themselves and encouraging their children to be so. There are numbers of 'criminal families' known to the police, in which parents are in and out of prison and the children follow the pattern of community home, detention centre, youth custody, prison.

- **poverty**, which makes the temptation to steal necessities high. Nearly 3 million people live on or below the poverty line, and 7 million people live on supplementary benefit.

- **personal 'inadequacy'**   People who are emotionally or mentally disturbed may not know the difference between right and wrong, and sometimes are not totally responsible for their actions. Often they need help rather than punishment. Some teenagers are easily led, weak-willed and lonely, and drift into crime because of pressure from others. The natural bully will steal from children in the playground or mug an old person for a few coins.

- **the social problems of our time** which include pressures that produce a high divorce rate and split families; materialistic attitudes; lack of parental guidance; and poor discipline. These all help to establish insecurity and lack of confidence in the young and can lead to antisocial behaviour.

- **faults in the education system**   Schools in which discipline is poor, there is a high truancy rate, and expectation of achievement is low, must bear some of the responsibility for the juvenile crime rate.

- **drug, alcohol and solvent abuse**   Young people can obtain these substances fairly easily and once hooked they can be driven to a life of crime to pay for their addiction. The figures shown below indicate that there has been a steep rise in the use of these substances since 1979.

Deaths associated with solvent abuse

	1979	**1984**
Total (England and Wales)	*12*	*58*

Source: *Hansard 1985*

Persons found guilty of or cautioned for drug offences

	1979	**1984**
Total (UK)	*14 339*	*25 022*
Under 17	*214*	*707*
17–20	*3 185*	*6 462*

Source: *Home Office Statistical Bulletin 1985*

In the late teens and early twenties, alcohol consumption is 40–50 per cent above the national average, with a high incidence of drunkenness. In 1983 more than 5000 young people under 18 were convicted of drunkenness. In the 13–16 age group, about one third of children drink at least once a week, but generally in small amounts. Drug and alcohol abuse in the late teens–early twenties age group is responsible for a high percentage of crimes such as petty theft, vandalism, violence, mugging and driving offences.

Juvenile crime

Juvenile crimes of violence (that is, those committed by 10–17-year-olds) and those committed by young people (17–21-year-olds) more than trebled from 1969 to 1983; many more cases go unreported. How are these young offenders dealt with?

In 1979, the number of 14–20-year-olds sentenced to immediate custody was 24 900; in 1984, the number was 30 500. Of the 1984 total, about 19 600 were sentenced to youth custody, and about 10 900 got detention centre orders.

Over two-thirds of the teenagers who are sentenced reappear in court shortly after leaving a penal establishment. (Borstals as a place of corrective punishment were abolished in the UK in 1983 and replaced by youth custody.) Many sociologists believe that custody is ineffective and other methods should be used. Some young offenders are put on probation, or into residential care; or they may be given an official caution, a suspended sentence, or a certain number of hours of community service work.

Some people think that a more positive approach is needed to help young offenders and suggestions include:

- Youth Training Projects to give young people better opportunities for jobs – with less free time for wrongdoing.
- phone-in services for youngsters in trouble, at risk, or in need of help.
- long-term residential care with specialised fostering available.
- intermediate treatment centres sponsored by the NCH to show youngsters why their behaviour is unacceptable and how to avoid future trouble.

Case history: *A day in the life of a young offender receiving custodial treatment*

This account is based on a real offender's experience.

I knew I might get put away because it was the second time I'd been to court, but I knew another kid who had a conditional discharge for what I'd done. I think what counted against me was that I hadn't been to school. I bunked off all last term.

When the Magistrate said I was going to D.C. [detention centre] for three months I was a bit choked. A guy in the next street had been and he said it was tough at first but he kept out of trouble and got full remission; he only did eight weeks. My solicitor said it would be a waste of time appealing.

The police took me straight down; they just let me say 'tara' to me mum. Then we got in the police car and drove straight off.

We got there just before 3 o'clock. The barbed wire was fifteen feet high.

The first few days were grim. Up at 6.30, drill on the yard, in for a shower, then cleaning, breakfast at 7.45. After breakfast I had more drill and because I was still at school I went to the classrooms from 9.00 a.m. to 12.00. In for dinner and then drill till 2 o'clock. I worked in the gardens or did sweeping in the afternoon. Tea at 4.30 and then we had about half an hour free time – we sat at tables and read books. 6.15 we had evening classes in the classroom until 7.45. There was Art, PE, Woodwork, Metalwork, Maths, English, Drama. Teachers came in from outside, it was all right. After that we had tea and a slice of bread and butter and we were in bed by 9.00 and the lights were out before 10.00.

The worst thing was parades, you were lining up all the time and being checked. You could only write one letter a week and it was checked. You could get permission to write another letter if your dad was away from home. You weren't allowed to write to your mates. You were allowed one visit from your mum a month.

They had grades, you started at the bottom and the staff gave you marks each week. You could earn up to 50p a week on the top grade and you had more privileges like better duties and extra PE. The officers were mostly all right if you didn't step out of line. You couldn't smoke and some of the lads had been on drugs and they had it rough without them.

I counted every day off; the worst thing was seeing other lads going out. I got all my remission. That was the day when I got my own clothes back and walked down the drive and I could see the other lads still working.

While I was there I said I'd never get into trouble again and I am still trying.

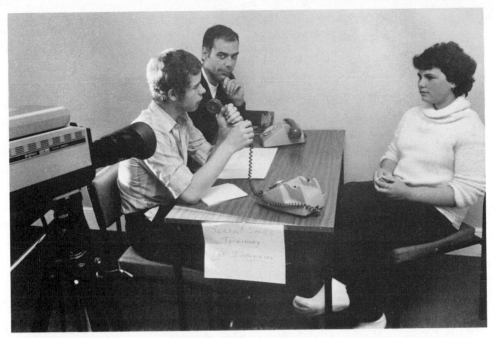

Non-custodial treatment centres like this are increasingly used by magistrates and local authorities in preference to the short, sharp shock.

Effects on the child

In some cases the whole family needs to be rehabilitated to break the vicious circle of family crime. Children who live in families where mother, father, siblings or relations are in trouble with the law can be severely affected. This pattern can be set up: the child is in trouble; the child is taken into care; the teenager is involved in more trouble and sentenced to youth custody; the teenager moves from petty crime to serious crime and is sentenced to prison.

Short-term effects include:

- the emotional difficulties of living with just one parent if the other is in prison, possibly resulting in neglect, child abuse, and/or insecurity.
- housing and/or financial problems if parents are not earning, resulting in insufficient shelter, food, warmth, clothing, etc.
- feelings of shame, guilt, and concern that other children may find out.
- antagonism from neighbours, and not being able to socialise with some children.
- conflicting loyalties within the family and between family and community.
- constant fear that family members who are involved in crime may get found out; having to live a life of deceit.

Long-term effects include:

- difficulty in forming relationships in later life, because of having an unsatisfactory father/mother figure.

57

- permanent psychological damage due to emotional stress.
- physical ill health due to neglect and deprivation.
- the child following the same criminal career.
- antisocial attitudes, and a narrow circle of friends.

Adults who are in charge of children's upbringing should teach them to be totally honest, the best way being by personal example. Children should know that stealing a sweet from a sister or brother, smashing a toy when in a temper, using unpleasant language, etc. are all unacceptable types of behaviour, and parents should realise that these small acts can lead to much more serious ones if left unchecked.

There should be no 'dual standards', such as expecting children to be honest while parents fiddle their tax returns or steal from where they work. Children will accept the standards and examples set by their parents.

Crimes against children

Many people feel that the worst possible crimes and the worst type of criminal are those involved with child abuse. It is a natural human instinct to protect the young, and many people find it difficult to understand how others can be cruel to children.

Child abuse can be divided into these areas:
- active physical ill-treatment resulting in temporary or permanent damage (non-accidental injury).
- mental and emotional ill-treatment resulting in psychological damage.
- neglect, deliberate or unintentional.
- sexual abuse.

The majority of cases of child cruelty take place in the home; sexual offences are usually committed by a father, stepfather, male relation or friend of the family. It is difficult to estimate the number of cases of child abuse that take place, as for every case reported, it is likely that many more remain undetected. NSPCC figures reveal that more than one child dies every week at the hands of parents or guardians, and 50 000 other children suffer varying forms of abuse. The Childline (0800 1111), set up in October 1986 to give abused children the chance of contacting a caring adult and getting help, received several thousand calls within a few hours of its start.

Even when a child may have been physically or mentally abused, and the case brought to court, she may be returned home. She will, however, be placed on the 'at risk' list and given constant social services monitoring.

The pictures opposite show some of the dreadful cruelties, appalling living conditions and moral dangers which children face. It is to be expected that they will carry the scars for the rest of their lives. (The causes and results of this subject are dealt with in Section C.)

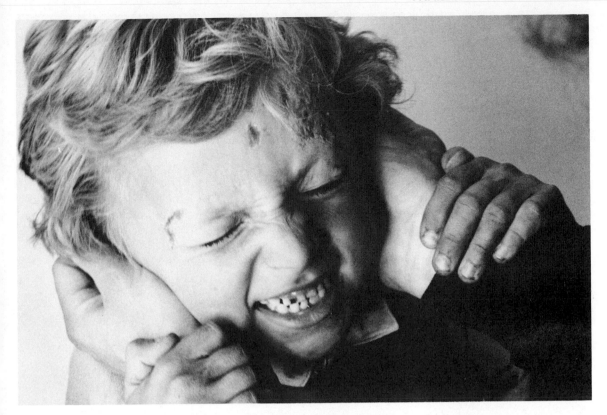

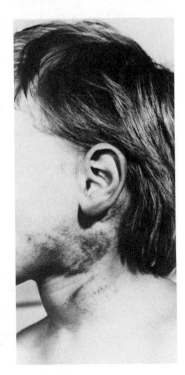

5 The Alternative Family

Children in local authority care

It is sometimes necessary for children to be taken away from their parents or guardians and put in the care of the local authority. There are many reasons for doing this but it is only done as a last resort. It is believed now that a child is better in his own home with his own family, rather than in a children's home, and if necessary the family is given training and support.

The local authority has a statutory responsibility to provide permanent or temporary residential accommodation for any child in need of care and protection. There are two main kinds of care:

- **voluntary care**   This is care for which no court order has been made.

- **compulsory care**   This is care by virtue of a court order or resolution.

Voluntary care

A child cannot be taken into care against a parent's wishes; voluntary care is often a temporary stay with the aim of returning the child to his home eventually. Often a foster home is used.

These are the main reasons for children being taken into voluntary care in 1984:

Reason	Number of children
Short-term illness of parent or guardian	2148
Long-term illness of parent or guardian	2119
Confinement of mother	185
Family homeless (eviction or other cause)	689
Parents dead (no guardian)	682
Abandoned or lost	1629
Death of one parent – other parent unable to cope	1695
Deserted by parent (includes illegitimate)	6077
Parent or guardian in prison	732
Unsatisfactory home conditions	7190
Other reasons	7744

Source: *DHSS*

Parents must be told where their children are and should be able to visit them. A parent can ask for a child to be returned and can only be deprived of the child if a court order is obtained and the local authority assumes parental rights.

Compulsory care

Care proceedings can be brought in the juvenile court by the local authority, the police, the NSPCC, or the local education authority, with the purpose of obtaining a **care order**, which will place the child in the care of the local authority, who then assume parental rights. The reasons and numbers for 1984 are shown below.

Reason	Number
Neglect or ill-treatment	*15 684*
Neglect or ill-treatment of another child in the household	*1 763*
Member of household convicted of an offence against children	*197*
Moral danger	*917*
Beyond parental control	*2 651*
Not receiving efficient full-time education	*2 603*
Guilty of an offence	*7 586*
In place of supervision order	*1 309*
Transfer of care order	*38*
Others	*2 935*

Source: *DHSS*

The courts can also make a **supervision order**, under which a child remains with the parents but is under the supervision of a social worker who will regularly visit to give care and advice.

A care order can last until the child is eighteen, when he is considered to be an adult. Parents should be able to have access to the child and can appeal to the juvenile court every six months to have the situation reviewed.

The total number of children in care in the UK in 1983 was 104 628. In 1977, 7.5 children were in care per 1000 population in the UK (11.3 in Scotland), and in 1983, the figures were 7.0 children per 1000 population in the UK (11.8 in Scotland). The highest regional number in 1983 was 8.2 (the North West).

Ages of children in care in England and Wales, 1983

Aged under 5	*9 169*
5–15	*54 598*
16 and over	*22 735*

Source: *DHSS*

61

These numbers give us the statistical picture of children who are unable to live with their natural parents in their own homes, but they do not show the amount of suffering caused to the children and the parents when they have to be separated. The decline of the extended family means that many families do not have relations to help them through their problems. Many families are now more isolated than they used to be because of: a higher proportion of families where both parents go out to work and therefore see little of the neighbours; more single-parent families who cannot maintain social contact with relatives and neighbours because of financial problems; the privacy of houses and flats; and the attitude of 'keeping yourself to yourself', which means that the support and influence of good neighbours is less apparent. Many children are now taken into care when previously they would have been cared for by relatives or kindly neighbours until the family problems were sorted out.

Some of the cases of neglect, minor child abuse, abandoned children, etc., can be helped by tackling the root of the problem, which may be poverty, ill health, stress, loneliness, ignorance or the need for practical help; and then the families will not need to be split up.

The effect of separating a child from his home and family – even a bad home and family – is likely to be traumatic. He may feel rejected, different from other children, unloved and bewildered. This will show in his immediate behaviour, either in the form of aggression, bullying, petty thieving, constant attention-seeking, rudeness and antisocial behaviour, or in a silent withdrawal with symptoms of emotional problems. The effects may be long lasting and result in inability to form lasting personal relationships and eventual neglect and cruelty to his own spouse and children. This well-known sequence costs a great deal in both suffering and finance; it can cost over £100 a week to keep a child in residential care, and this money would be better spent on helping the families in trouble.

The foster child

Fostering is seen as a very good alternative to placing children in residential homes and these are some of the advantages:

- It can provide family care for children if they cannot be with their own families.

- It can be used for short- or long-term placements.

- It does not have the commitment of adoption.

- It avoids children becoming institutionalised.

- The right kind of foster parents can give warmth and affection without being too demanding.

- It enables 'difficult' children, e.g. those with behavioural problems, handicapped children, or older children, the chance to experience home life.

The dangers of fostering can include:

- foster parents with the wrong motivation, e.g. those who do it only for the money, those who become too possessive, and those who neglect or ill-treat the child.

- the degree of failure. If a child fails to settle into the foster home, or is rejected by his foster parents, this is yet another failure or loss for him – a 'double deprivation' – and provides even more suffering for the child.
- several changes of foster home, brought about when foster parents cannot continue to keep the child, or the child does not like or cannot get on with the foster parents.
- a strong attachment formed between child and foster parent, and resulting distress if and when the natural parents decide to take the child back. A few foster placements eventually result in adoption.

Many children's homes throughout the country have been closed as the fostering scheme has extended, and it is of course much cheaper to foster a child than to keep him in residential accommodation; but a well-run, small residential unit can be very good, and may be preferable for some children needing special care.

Foster parents do not have any legal rights and must return the child to the natural parents or the local authority when requested to do so. They are paid a sum of money (boarding out allowance) to cover the maintenance of the child and an extra allowance for holidays, pocket money and special needs. The local authority pays this money and each authority sets its own rate of payment. Some authorities employ specialist foster parents to care for 'problem' children – those with behaviour problems or handicaps, young offenders, etc. – for which they receive special payment.

Training sessions are normally available for both types of foster parents, and group meetings are often arranged so that the more experienced foster parents can help and guide newer ones.

There are certain regulations for foster parents and they must agree to:
- allow the local authority to visit.
- care for the child's health.
- look after him in the same way as their own children.
- give the child up upon request
- bring the child up in his own religion and culture.

Foster parents need to:
- love children and enjoy looking after them.
- be prepared to share their love with someone else's child and not discriminate.
- be physically healthy, and be mentally and emotionally stable and secure.
- treat the work professionally and not become too emotionally involved.
- be mature in outlook and have sensible ideas about discipline, feeding, etc.
- be prepared to seek and accept training and advice.
- have a sufficiently large home, preferably with a garden, to accommodate one or more children comfortably.

- realise that fostering is not a short cut to adoption and is in fact regarded very differently by the care authorities.

Foster parents will be expected to encourage liaison with the child's natural parent(s), aiming eventually to bring the family together again.

The adopted child

Adoption is a legal undertaking with all the responsibilities of caring for a natural child – it is for people, usually couples, who really want to bring a child into their lives and the lives of any other children they have. It is important, therefore, that people who are planning to adopt a child consider their own motives first. Adoption societies will question prospective adoptive parents closely and will counsel them to wait or reconsider if they think their motives are not sound enough. The process is one of finding suitable parents for babies, not finding babies for parents; the child is the most important consideration.

People considering adoption should therefore remember:

- a child will not mend a failing marriage; a baby may add extra problems.
- the child is entitled to a secure, loving home background, which is financially sound.
- the new parents should have some experience with children and be mature enough to realise their responsibilities.
- some couples may be too old, e.g. over forty, to cope with very young children.
- a child should not be adopted just as a replacement for a child who has died; he should be wanted for his own sake.
- if there are other children in the family they also should be consulted; it is unfair if they feel pushed out, and the newcomer should not be made to feel unwanted by the other children.
- many adoption agencies prefer to place a child in a family of the same ethnic group.

In 1971, there were 23 000 adoptions in Britain; in 1983, there were 10 000; and in 1984, there was a further drop. These figures show a drop of more than half, not because people do not wish to adopt, but because the babies are not available. This is due to:

- fewer unwanted babies being born, because of better contraceptive measures and easier access to abortion.
- single mothers being given advice, support and encouragement to keep their child.
- less social disapproval of illegitimacy.

Fewer than 800 babies under six months old and fewer than 2000 under a year old were adopted in 1984. There is a much greater chance of being able to adopt an older child – there are an estimated 20 000 children in care suitable for adoption. People can consider adopting children of school age, siblings who wish to stay together, or special cases such as a child with a physical or mental handicap.

People who wish to adopt must apply to an approved adoption agency. This may be run by the local authority or by a voluntary organisation such as the National Children's Home. Private adoptions can only be made by a member of the child's family. A legal adoption is permanent; it cannot be reversed, and a new birth certificate will be issued when the adoption is confirmed.

Prospective adoptive parents must be:

- over 21 years old.
- (if two people apply) usually a married couple – a single male or female may be considered for an older child, and homosexual couples may be considered.
- medically examined.
- under 35 years old, usually, if female.
- approved by the adoption agency.

If an adoption agency approves the parents and they have a suitable child available, the child will live for at least 3 months with the family, with supervision from a social worker who will make reports and recommendations for the court hearing. The child's natural parents and the child himself (if old enough) will also be consulted. An adoption order cannot be approved without one or both of the natural parents' consent. At an official hearing the court will decide if it is in the child's best interests for the adoption to go forward, and if the court decides it is, the adoption order will be issued.

All adoptions do not end happily. The adopted child, especially if he is older or has special difficulties, may find it hard to settle down; the new parents may have difficulties if the child is naughty or emotionally upset; other children in the family may be jealous. It needs patience and understanding, and the adoption societies offer post-adoption advice when requested.

The big problem may arise when the child is told that he is adopted. Many parents do not like telling the child and the child may respond in a variety of ways. Since the Children's Act (1975), adopted children have had the right to have access to their original birth certificate at the age of eighteen. In this way they may be able to trace their natural parents. This can be a very rewarding experience, or it can be a great shock to both parties.

With your group discuss the advantages and the dangers of allowing adopted children to be able to trace their natural parents.

Agencies which help:
- British Agencies for Adoption and Fostering (BAAF), 11 Southwark Street, London SE1 1RQ   They issue an annual guide, 'Adopting a child', and a leaflet, 'Talking about origins'.
- The Post-adoption Support Centre, Gregory House, 48 Mecklenburgh Square, London WC1N 2NU.

Homes run by voluntary agencies

As well as the residential homes run by the local authorities, there are also those which are established and run by voluntary agencies. Many of these were founded during the nineteenth century by individuals such as Dr Barnardo, by church organisations such as the Church of England Children's Society, by those seeking to help with specific problems such as blindness, or by charitable trusts founded by important industrialists such as Seebohm Rowntree. These homes are financed through voluntary contributions and government assistance. Local authorities use these homes to place children in need, and they must be registered and open for inspection by central government to make sure they maintain proper standards. The old idea of the 'orphanage for poor children' has gone; voluntary societies aim to provide small residential groups with accommodation to suit their special needs. Their aims include 'whole family' care and uniting a family after as short a separation time as possible. Many of them have fostering and adoption agencies, and place as many children with families as possible.

Following this are some facts about some of the organisations. You can find out more by writing for information to any of the voluntary societies, or even by offering your help.

- **Church of England Children's Society**   Founded in 1881, and then known as the 'Waifs and Strays', the Society now has at least 44 residential establishments in England and Wales and helps over 50 000 children and their families every year. They also run day care centres, family centres and holiday schemes, and concentrate on preventative work and self help.

- **Dr Barnardo's**   Dr Barnado founded his first home for destitute boys in London in 1870. The society aims to provide specialised residential, educational or day care for use by local authorities and social services; and to carry out experimental work and projects which concentrate on preventative measures.

- **National Children's Bureau**   The Bureau does not run children's homes, but brings together all the information needed by professionals such as social workers, teachers, etc., and by the children and families in need of help. They have an extensive information service and conduct special enquiries.

- **National Children's Homes**   Founded in 1869 to help children and families in need, by providing homes and hostels, they now have over 120 differing centres of work. These include sixteen residential centres, thirteen adolescent independence units, seventeen homes and schools for physically and mentally handicapped children, thirteen family centres, etc. They train large numbers of people in the caring skills and are active in helping children at risk.

- **Royal National Institute for the Blind**   Founded in 1868 to help blind people in the UK, they have a large network of 'sunshine homes', hostels, training and recreational centres and residential schools to provide help and accommodation for the visually handicapped. They also provide services such as literature in Braille, 'talking books' (books recorded on audio-tape), etc.

- **Royal Society for Mentally Handicapped Children and Adults (MENCAP)**   Founded in 1946 to help the handicapped and their families, they now have three residential centres for young adults and four other residential homes for younger children; but much of their work involves educating the general public to the needs of handicapped people.

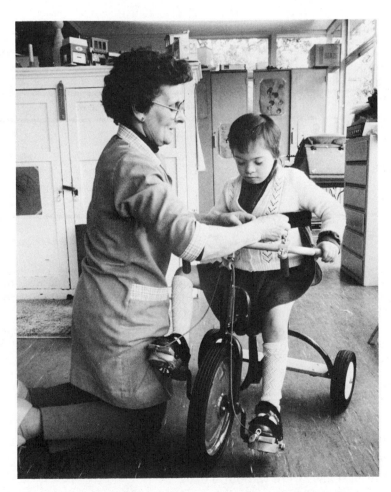

Alexandra House, one of the NCH's residental homes

Alexandra House is set in the London suburb of Ealing. It could be called a residential nursery, a re-habilitation centre, a home for multiple-handicapped young children, a hospice. It is all these things, but above all, it is a home to its 18 children, mostly under five years of age, who are in need of love, security, and healing of body and soul.

So many people still think of us caring for orphans, without realising the complex situations from which our children are admitted, and the pain they have experienced already in their young lives. Although our main responsibility is the care of the children, we are continually working with families, trying to reconcile, to rehabilitate, even if that proves impossible at a later stage.

Source: *Children, Summer 1986*

6 Family Finance

Financial problems are one of the major factors which contribute to family quarrels and marital breakdown. It is essential to be able to plan your money, budget carefully and be a wise shopper, whatever your income. Children should be taught from an early age how to look after money and be given opportunities to manage their own financial affairs.

Income

The table below compares the average income for the UK in 1983 with that of some other countries.

Country	Average yearly income
UK	£9550
Holland	£9500
Italy	£7900
Costa Rica	£2250
Bangladesh	£370

Source: *Encyclopaedia Britannica 1986*

It is difficult to make true comparisons with other countries where much of the population work their own piece of land to feed them, where the climate is such that they do not need to heat their homes, and where expectations are different. In this country many household appliances are considered necessities, and many 'luxury' items are owned by a high proportion of households.

In the UK (1983-4):

94 per cent of homes owned a refrigerator and TV.

41 per cent of council tenants owned a deep freeze.

70 per cent of owner occupiers owned a deep freeze.

Only 2 per cent of homes were without a bath.

Over 75 per cent of homes had a telephone.

64 per cent of homes had central heating.

66 per cent of people had had holidays abroad.

20 per cent of people took a second holiday each year.

61 per cent of households owned a car.

15 per cent had the use of two or more cars.

These facts show that many families have a very comfortable standard of living. Family income is usually obtained from the wage or salary of members of the household plus any social security benefits to which they are entitled, such as child benefit, attendance allowances, etc. (see Section D, 'Community Care and Provision').

The average weekly earnings for 1980 were £111.40; for 1985, £171.70. In 1984, the average weekly earnings of manual workers were: male, £159.30; female, £97.33. The weekly earnings obviously vary according to the type of occupation of the employee.

Types of employment

The chart below shows how earnings differed between manual and non-manual workers and male and female workers in Britain in 1984.

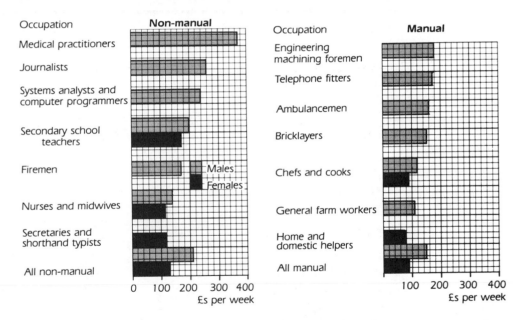

Average gross weekly earnings of full-time employees in selected occupation groups in Britain, April 1984: by sex

Source: *Social Trends 1986*

Information from the General Household Survey is used by the government to produce the **socioeconomic groupings**, which classify the country's population into groups according to the type of work performed and the income received from it.

Socioeconomic groupings

	Definition	**Example**
Group 1	*Professional*	*Doctor*
Group 2	*Employers and managers, administrative*	*Secondary school teacher*
Group 3	*Intermediate and junior non-manual*	*Shorthand typist*
Group 4	*Skilled manual*	*Engineering foreman*
Group 5	*Semiskilled manual and personal service*	*Postman*
Group 6	*Unskilled manual*	*Labourer*

Expenditure

Average family spending

1984	£151.92 a week (£57.97 a head)
1983	£141.03 a week
1953–4	£21.25 a week

Source: Department of Employment survey, 1984

This chart gives an idea of how the average family spent its income in 1984.

Average family weekly spending, 1984

Source: *Department of Employment survey, 1984*

Low income and its effects

Because of the high level of unemployment (see p. 21), there are many families who must manage with a great deal less than some of the figures shown above. More than half a million British children are in families where the chief wage earner has been unemployed for two or more years, and there are 1 250 000 young people living in homes with unemployed parents.

These families, unless they have savings or a private source of income, must live on supplementary benefits. A basic supplementary benefit for a couple with two primary school aged children in 1984 was £68.05 per week. This is well below the average family expenditure in 1984 shown on p. 70. In 1948, one person in 33 was dependent on supplementary benefit; in August 1983, the figure was one in eight. Other types of family who tend to be living on or below the poverty line are single-parent families, families with a child or adult with a handicap, and some elderly people.

Life can be very bleak and depressing living in the circumstances shown in the photographs here, and there is a high percentage of divorce, marital problems, child abuse, and other social problems, amongst families living in poverty. Several voluntary societies work hard to help low income families, and campaign for better allowances and living conditions from government sources. One such society is the Child Poverty Action Group, founded in 1965, which produces some valuable statistical information and welfare benefit guides.

Cost of child rearing

Before couples decide to have a child, it is worth noting that a report by the Family Policy Centre found that it can cost £30 000 to bring up a child from birth to the age of 16. This does not allow for the loss of one parent's income if he or she gives up work to care for the child. It does include £755 for initial outlay on baby clothing and equipment, and £28–£56 for feeding, clothing and heating per week (1986 figures).

Consumer advice and protection

Whatever the family income, household expenditure should be carefully planned to:

- get value for money.
- provide the necessities first.
- avoid expensive mistakes.
- avoid getting into debt.
- take advantage of consumer protection.

Getting value for money

To get value for money it is necessary to know:

- what you want to buy,
- what you want the article to do,
- what you can afford to pay,
- the choice available for that article, and
- the shops which stock the article.

You therefore need to do some spadework and some planning before you start. For regular weekly shopping for food, toiletries, stationery, inexpensive items of clothing, etc., keep a regular check on prices, compare the adverts in the newspapers, free papers, teletext, and window displays, and use the shops which regularly have reduced prices in the items you buy – but buy quality goods and named varieties, as cheap ones often don't wear well, have a poor flavour, break easily, etc.

Get to know your shops and use the ones which give good, reliable service, stock high quality goods and replace faulty goods willingly.

When buying more expensive items such as electrical goods, furniture, etc., use the shop's catalogue of prices or their newspaper adverts, or ring them up for prices. You can save several pounds by shopping around.

Providing the necessities first

Some families get into debt or are poorly fed, clothed and housed, because they do not follow the basic rule of 'necessities first, luxuries if they can be afforded'. People who are easily tempted should:

- make a shopping list and stick to it.
- only take sufficient money with them to buy what they have planned – leave the rent money, etc. at home.
- try to budget their money, and have a sensible weekly or monthly housekeeping account to cover essentials.
- pay bills promptly before they have the chance to spend the cash on other items. Sometimes a discount is given for prompt payment of bills.
- set aside some savings to allow for the occasional luxury item.

Avoiding expensive mistakes

Most of us have expensive garments hanging unworn in our wardrobes because they were impulse buys, or household gadgets we never use because they are too complicated, or children have toys they never play with because the person who bought them made a poor choice. These things all waste money.

Some of the following points can help to avoid such expensive mistakes:

- When buying clothing take along a reliable friend, but don't be persuaded just because they like it. Don't let an overenthusiastic salesperson influence you, don't buy it just because it's a bargain, and don't think it will suit you better when you get it home or that the colour is a 'good enough' match – all these things lead to unused clutter in your wardrobe.
- Don't buy garments for yourself or for children which are very delicate and will constantly need drycleaning.
- Don't pay a lot of money for a fashion which will soon pass or something very dramatic which you will soon tire of.
- Don't buy an expensive kitchen gadget when it is quicker and easier to do the job by hand.
- Bulk buying of foods may save money, but only if they will all get eaten before the family are tired of them.

Avoiding getting into debt

It is very easy to obtain credit these days and some families soon find that their outgoings are far exceeding their income.

Banks offer

Overdrafts	*For larger sums of money*
Personal loans	*For a car, washing machine, home improvement, etc.*
Credit cards (such as Barclaycard, Access)	*Available to people over eighteen – a high interest rate is charged and a large debt can soon be run up*

Stores offer

Their own credit cards (as do Marks and Spencer, Debenhams, etc.)	*The cards can only be used in the one store – it may be tempting to buy unnecessary items and interest rates may be high*
Extended terms	*With extended terms the cost can be spread over three months without interest*
Hire-purchase terms	*Hire-purchase may be for several years but the interest will be high*

Mail order

Many things can now be purchased through a catalogue and the payments spread over 40 weeks	*A tempting way to buy; often it is too much trouble to return goods which are not quite suitable or a bit faulty; tends to be more expensive*

It is often very useful to be able to have the use of expensive goods and spread the payments over several months or years. The cost of the article may have gone up in price during that time anyway, but the purchaser should always:

- check the amount of interest he or she is paying.
- be sure he or she can afford the repayments. Often the article can be repossessed if the instalments are not paid regularly.
- check that he or she is covered by the guarantee for repairs and servicing or replacement if the article is faulty.

If in serious difficulties because of sudden unemployment, serious illness, etc., it is worth explaining the situation to the lender (bank, shop, credit company, etc.), who may be able to defer payments. The social services may be able to help and the Citizens' Advice Bureau (CAB) will give advice.

Taking advantage of consumer protection

Being a good shopper is not enough; you must also know how the law protects you from unscrupulous salespeople, and remember that shopkeepers have rights too – they are not compelled to take an article back just because you don't like it when you get home. You need to know the laws regarding:

- a straightforward sales transaction,
- second-hand goods
- door-to-door selling,
- unsolicited goods,
- buying a car,
- the value of guarantees,
- having work done for you, and
- insurance cover.

The law says that goods must be:

- of *merchantable quality*, that is, they must not be damaged or broken.
- *fit for their purpose* and do the job they are intended for.
- *as they are described*, either on the packet, in display or verbally by the seller.

If the goods do not measure up to these three rules then the seller has broken the contract and the buyer has a claim. This applies to goods bought in most ways, whether from shops, market traders, door-to-door, catalogues, or credit sales, and to hired goods and goods bought in sales. It does not, however, apply to second-hand goods, private sales or trading stamp transactions.

Purchases are covered by the Sale of Goods Act (1979, extended in 1982). The seller, not the manufacturer, is responsible for the goods he or she sells, under this Act, and can be sued if he or she breaks the law.

Other important consumer acts include:

- **Trade Descriptions Acts (1968 and 1972)**   This makes it a criminal offence to give a misleading description of any goods, and states that goods must bear an indication of their country of origin. Consumers should report any offence to their local Trading Standards Department, and the trader if guilty is liable to a fine or imprisonment.

- **Food Act (1984)**   This implemented a number of food hygiene and labelling regulations, and made it an offence to sell food unfit for human consumption or to have unclean food premises. Offences should be reported to the local environmental health officer.

- **Unsolicited Goods and Services Act (1971)** This makes it an offence to demand money for goods or a service which the customer has not had, or for goods sent unsolicited and not wanted. You do not have to pay for unsolicited goods and it is the responsibility of the sender to take them away. The person who receives the goods must keep them for six months; if the sender does not collect them within that time they become the property of the recipient. The Trading Standards Department deal with prosecutions.

- **Consumer Credit Act (1974)** This requires that the true price and the total amount of interest charged be told to the customer; that credit cannot be refused for reasons of sex or race; and that anyone refused credit can check the credit reference file for any untrue statements.

- **Consumer Protection Acts (1961/1971)** and the **Consumer Safety Act (1978)** These deal specifically with the safety of goods and allow for quick action to prohibit the sale of any unsafe articles, such as toys.

- **Consumer Protection Act (1987)** This makes it easier for consumers who are injured or have property damaged by faulty goods to obtain compensation. It also tightens up other loopholes and makes producers of goods much more liable for damage or injury.

Faulty goods

What do you do if you buy something which is not satisfactory?

The first thing to do is to return it to the shop or person who sold it to you. If the goods are faulty the seller will probably refund all or part of your money, or if you prefer, give you an exchange or a repair. The seller may offer a credit note, which you can refuse if you wish.

You will not, however, be automatically entitled to a refund or exchange if:

- you have obviously worn or used the article in such a way as to damage it through careless use.

- the goods were given to you as a present – the transaction was with the original buyer.

- you bought the goods knowing them to be faulty – on special offer or at reduced price.

- you changed your mind because the colour, fit, or taste was wrong.

The seller will often change the article in these circumstances, but he or she does not have to.

If the seller refuses a refund or exchange on grounds other than those given, ask to see someone, or write to someone, in authority, such as the shop manager or a sales manager. If necessary use the threat of a solicitor's letter. After this it is best to get advice from the CAB or a Consumers Advice Centre, who will advise you how to take out a summons in the Small Claims Court. This is simple and cheap to do, but usually the threat of it is sufficient to make a seller offer a settlement.

Sellers also have rights, and when they put goods on display and give a price they are only making an offer to the consumer. They need not:

- sell the goods to you at all.
- charge the price on the ticket.
- take articles out of the shop window.
- allow you into the shop.

In case you do need to make a complaint always make sure you keep your receipts, copies of any letters sent, and a note of the dates of any phone calls made and what was said.

Sources of help
The following people and organisations will help the consumer both in their choice of goods and to deal with complaints after purchase.

- **Central government departments**
  Department of the Environment
  Department of Trade
  Department of Energy
  Ministry of Agriculture, Fisheries and Food
  Office of Fair Trading – publishes consumer education material, stops unfair trading and prosecutes traders where necessary
  National Consumer Council – gives advice to official bodies; does not deal with individual complaints
  British Standards Institution – partly sponsored by the Government; issues booklets and other publications giving consumer guidelines and sets the standards for government regulations and the kitemark (issued when goods produced are in accordance with a British Standard)

- **Local government departments**
  Environmental Health Department – deals with food and water pollution, housing, environmental hazards, etc.
  Trading Standards Department – deals with weights and measures, safety, and other consumer complaints
  Consumer Advice Centres – usually situated in busy shopping centres or maybe a mobile van to give on-the-spot advice to shoppers; but many local authorities have closed them because of economic cuts

- **Voluntary and independent organisations**
  Citizens' Advice Bureau
  Consumers' Association – gives general advice to the public but caters mainly for members; publishes *Which?*
  Coal, electricity, gas, solid fuel, law – all have centres or councils which give literature and advice

- **The media**
  The media also provide a lot of useful, topical and interesting information and guidance in the form of special TV programmes, radio programmes, TV advertising, magazine surveys on domestic equipment, cars, etc.

How good are you as a shopper? (Answers are on p. 85.)

1 Has a salesperson the right to knock at your door and offer goods for sale?

2 Can you insist on having a receipt for anything you purchase?

3 An article in the window is marked at one price but is marked at a higher price inside the shop. Can you insist on having it at the shop window price?

4 You buy a handbag which the label says is made of leather. When you get it home you find it is plastic. Which law has been broken?

5 Which of these drinks contains the most fruit?
  Fruit drink
  Fruit squash or cordial
  Orangeade

6 You receive some Christmas cards through the post from a well-known charity. They suggest you pay a certain sum of money. What should you do?

7 You go to the hairdressers for a perm, and the hairdresser ruins your hair. What can you do?

8 The transistor radio you buy (in a box, at the correct price) does not work when you get it home. What are your rights?

9 The restaurant where you have a meal charges you 12 per cent service charge. Is this correct?

10 Your niece pulls the head off the doll which you bought her for Christmas, and you see a long sharp spike which was used to hold the head in place. What should you do?

Summary and Evaluation

This section helps to put the family into perspective. Children need a secure and loving home background, and couples should think about this before they plan to have a family. Family life cannot always be perfect but children will learn from their parents, siblings and relatives how to behave and how to fit into the community. Sometimes children's experiences at home are so bad that they will react with antisocial behaviour; sometimes they will be scarred physically or mentally for life. If home circumstances are unbearable or difficult, children may have to be placed elsewhere, but this is only as a last resort. There are no clear definitions of a 'bad' home or a 'good' home; very often living in a slum with parents who ill-treat them is more acceptable to children than being taken away to live with strangers. Finance is a very important factor; even families with an adequate income will be in financial difficulties if they do not know how to budget effectively, and the law must protect families against the sharp practices or overpersuasiveness of some retailers.

Follow-up Work

Fact finding exercises

1 Find out and explain the meaning of the following terms:
sibling rivalry
the kibbutz system
egocentric
socialisation
materialistic society

2 List the signs which could identify the isolated, rejected child and which could lead you to suspect child abuse.

3 What is the difference between:
polyandry and polygyny?
indictable and non-indictable offences?
adoption and fostering?
introvert and extrovert?

Problem solving exercises

1 It is sometimes difficult for different age groups within a family to live together. Suggest ways in which the situations below can be resolved.

2 Suggest how:
   a) parents could help a 4–5-year-old child who is having difficulty making friends.

   b) a teenager, who has just moved with his or her family into a new area, can make contact with youngsters of his or her own age group.

   c) a playgroup leader can involve the parents as well as the children in the group's activities.

   d) an active, newly retired person can interest himself or herself in, and be of help to, the community.

3 Study the list of aims for the parents of an only child on p. 35. Suggest ways in which some of these could be achieved (such as joining a mother and toddler group).

4 *Situation*   Jenny went on a day visit to a town some distance away. While there she saw a blouse in a shop window and bought it on the spur of the moment.

   Problem   This was an impulse buy. Jenny did not try it on in the shop and found when she tried it on at home that it was too tight and did not go with anything else in her wardrobe.

   Possible solutions   Jenny could:
   a) wait until she visited the town again and then try to exchange the blouse or get a refund.

   b) try to alter the blouse to fit her, and buy a new skirt to match.

c) try to sell it to, or swop it with, a thinner friend or relation.

d) do some exercises and go on a slimming course.

e) give it to someone for Christmas.

f) put the blouse at the back of her wardrobe until she got thinner and bought a new skirt.

How would *you* solve the problem?

Which of the above alternatives would you favour?

Free response questions

1 How and why should the methods used for disciplining a young child be different from those used for a teenager?

Suggest some possible effects upon a young child of over-strict or over-lenient discipline.

2 Explain and give your opinions upon this statement: 'Parents are born not made'.

Activities

1 Do a survey of the people in your class to find out about their place in the family and how they feel about it. Ask them the following questions:

i) What is your place in the family?

ii) Have you ever wished you were the youngest/oldest/only one, etc.?

iii) What problems have you found connected with your position in the family?

iv) What advantages does it bring?

2 There are many methods of shopping and types of shop. Study the chart opposite, make a copy in your book and fill it in to indicate your preferences. Some have been done to guide you.

Select four of the methods of shopping and compare them.

	Keen prices	Quick service	No sales pressure	Large choice of goods	Large choice of one type of merchandise	Friendly service	Credit available	Quality goods	Time to decide	No parking difficulties	Good after-service	No problem of taking children shopping
Corner shop						****	**					*
Supermarkets			****									
Hypermarket										****	***	
Chain stores				****				****				
Specialist shops					****							
Market stalls	****	***										
Home catalogue							****		****			
Product parties (e.g. Pippa Dee)								**	*			****

Key

****	Excellent
***	Good
**	Adequate
*	Poor
No stars	Unsatisfactory

3 Explain the illustration below. Why is it often easier to discipline someone else's child than for parents to do this for themselves?

Onlooker: If she was my child, I would give her a good smacking.

Mother: If she was *your* child, so would I.

Make another drawing to illustrate the subject of crime prevention and how to protect your property.

4 Make a family scrapbook; put in photographs, birthday cards, invitations, and a record of special events such as births, marriages and deaths. Ask your grandparents, aunts and uncles where they used to live and what it was like. Find out if any of your relations were killed during one of the world wars, or if any emigrated to other countries. Your own family are special; find out what you can about them.

You could include a family tree; if you are good at embroidery you could embroider one. It could look like this:

5   Find out if you have a system of community policing in your area. Do a survey to discover if people like to see a member of the police walking the beat.

Have you got a neighbourhood watch scheme in operation near you? If not, try to get your neighbours interested. The police will be only too pleased to give you and your family help and information.

Answers to consumer quiz on p. 78.

1   Yes. Anyone can knock at your door. You do not have to buy.

2   No. A shopkeeper need not give a receipt.

3   No. You cannot insist on buying anything at a particular price, but the shop should be reported as they are committing a criminal offence.

4   The Trade Descriptions Act.

5   *Fruit squash or cordial* contains 25 per cent before dilution. Fruit drink need only contain 10 per cent and orangeade need not contain any fruit at all.

6   The cards are yours if they are not claimed within six months. If it is for a good cause you could buy the cards as suggested and so help the charity.

7   If the hairdresser spoils the look of your hair he or she must refund your money and/or try to put the matter right.

8   A replacement radio or a complete refund.

9   Only if it is shown on the menu or if you are told about it before you order your meal.

10   Take the doll to your local Trading Standards Department (often at the Town Hall), the CAB, or a Consumer Advice Centre – it is a danger and should be reported.

SECTION C Handicapped Children and their Families

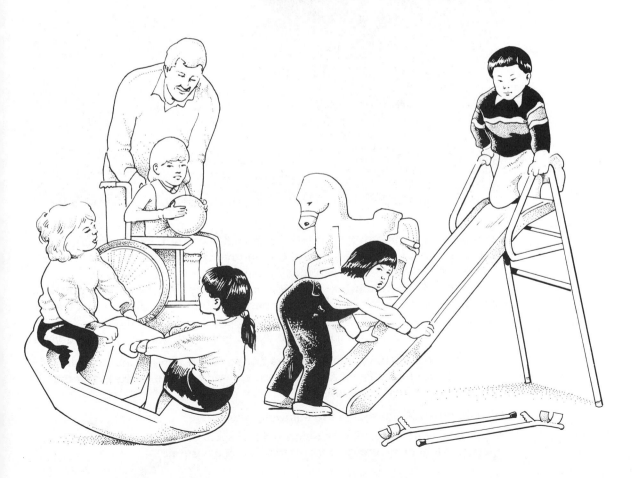

7 Handicap

Before the beginning of this century, many babies with mental or physical handicaps would not have survived during pregnancy, at the birth, or during the first few weeks of life. Even today many of the foetuses which are spontaneously aborted are found to be in some way defective; this produces a natural reduction in the numbers of imperfect babies born. But with increased medical knowledge and care, and better hygiene and community provision, many of the handicapped babies who would previously have died are surviving.

A **handicap** is anything which hinders normal development and normal living. It may be very minor (such as being short-sighted or slightly deaf), or it may be moderate, or it may be severe.

We can group handicaps in the following way:

● *physical handicaps* such as deformed limbs, *congenital handicaps* such as spina bifida or *severe chronic diseases* such as asthma.

- *mental handicaps* related to chromosomal conditions such as Down's syndrome, or to brain-damage conditions such as cerebral palsy. *Mentally retarded* children are slow to learn and slow to achieve their full mental potential.

- *sensory handicaps* such as disabilities in speech, hearing and sight.

- *emotional handicaps*. These can show themselves in many different ways, including physical or behaviour problems, and they may be much more difficult to identify than the previous handicap groups.

- *interrelated handicaps*. This is the term for a combination of handicaps, as in the Down's syndrome child who is both physically and mentally handicapped, or the physically deformed child who is also emotionally disturbed.

Deaf/blind children being taught

It is difficult to know the number of handicapped children in Britain, but it is probably about 10–15 per cent of all children.

Some figures:

- About four babies in every thousand born have a severe mental handicap, and many more are mildly affected.

- There are more than 137 000 full-time pupils receiving special education at schools for the physically or mentally handicapped.

- More than 50 000 handicapped children are looked after in their own homes by relatives.

- It costs up to £500 000 per lifetime to support a handicapped person.

These figures show that a great deal must be done to help to cut down the financial drain on society. A great deal of research is now carried out into the causes of handicap and from that should develop better ways of prevention.

The rest of this chapter is about the types of handicap shown in the following diagram.

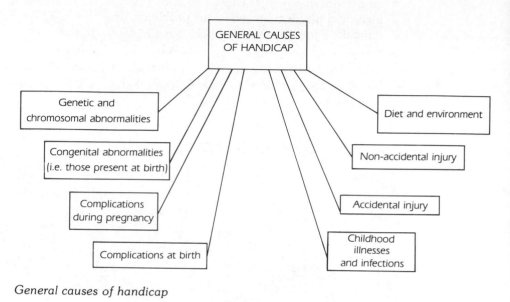

General causes of handicap

Genetic and chromosomal abnormalities

There are usually twenty-two pairs of chromosomes and two sex chromosomes found in the nucleus of each cell in the human body. These chromosomes carry the genes which dictate our characteristics.

In about 1 : 250 live births, chromosomal abnormalities occur that lead to serious physical and/or mental defects. One of these is Down's syndrome, caused by having an extra chromosome.

Many abnormalities are inherited through the genes; if any genes are faulty a defect can occur. This defect can be passed from generation to generation, or it may skip a generation and continue with the next one. These abnormalities include: galactosaemia, albinism, muscular dystrophy, cystic fibrosis, phenylketonuria (PKU), and sickle cell anaemia.

Some conditions are sex-linked; if a female has a single abnormal recessive gene she will be a **carrier** – she will not herself have the disease, but she will pass it on, usually to a male child. Such conditions include: haemophilia, some types of muscular dystrophy, colour blindness, and dwarfism.

Congenital abnormalities (those present at birth)

Most chromosomal abnormalities are present at birth, although they are not always detectable until the child is older. Very serious abnormalities which may be present at birth include spina bifida, hydrocephalus, anencephaly (where the skull is not completely formed – the baby usually dies), cerebral palsy, and major physical deformity. Others are much less serious, such as having an extra finger or toe. There may be slight to severe brain damage; defects to the heart, liver or kidneys; and/or disorders of the digestive tract.

A deformed foetus is often naturally aborted, but about thirty live births in every thousand have some form of abnormality.

Complications during pregnancy

There are several factors which can affect the foetus during its development in the womb, and possibly lead to a child being handicapped. Some of the factors can be controlled, such as smoking, diet, use of drugs etc.; but others are beyond the immediate control of the expectant mother, such as infections, environmental hazards, and accidents. The expectant mother may, however, be able to lessen the risks, and this is why good antenatal care is essential.

Controllable factors

- **Parents' relationship** Babies born to parents who are closely related (for example, first cousins) may be perfectly normal, but in some cases an inherited family disorder may be carried by both partners and passed on to the child.

- **Age of the mother** Congenital malformations are much more likely to occur when the mother is under 16 or over 40. A Down's syndrome baby is likely in only 1 in 2000 babies for most mothers, but the risk increases to 1 in 50 for mothers over 45.

- **Smoking** The expectant mother who continues to smoke during pregnancy puts her unborn child very much at risk. Statistical figures show that expectant mothers who smoke run a higher risk of having a premature (pre-term) baby, or a light birth weight baby, with all the resulting risks of these two conditions. There is also an indication that some malformations, such as hare lip, cleft palate, and congenital heart disease, are more common in the babies of mothers who smoke.

- **Alcohol** Heavy drinking during pregnancy can cause mental and physical damage to the foetus. The newborn babies of alcoholic mothers, like those of mothers who smoke, tend to be premature or of low birth weight. In the long term, it has been found that children of mothers who smoked and/or drank heavily during pregnancy tend to be less physically well developed and slower in intellectual development than others.

- **Drugs**   There is no doubt that taking drugs, unprescribed or prescribed, can be very dangerous to the foetus. Some antibiotics can cause kidney failure; LSD, cocaine and heroin can cause the baby to be addicted; antihistamines can cause deafness and jaundice.

  A drug prescribed as a sedative for expectant mothers in the 1960s, thalidomide, caused the birth of babies with gross physical deformities. Even aspirin can be dangerous if taken in regular large doses.

- **Vaccinations**   These must be avoided during pregnancy, especially the live vaccines such as those given for rubella, measles, polio, smallpox and TB, which can pass through the placenta and infect the foetus. The first fourteen weeks of pregnancy are the most dangerous period.

- **X-rays**   These should be avoided during the first four months of pregnancy, and other tests such as ultrasound should be used. If an X-ray is essential, the abdomen should be shielded by a lead apron. X-rays, which are a form of radiation, may damage the rapidly developing cells of the foetus.

- **Sexual infections**   Untreated sexually transmitted diseases such as gonorrhoea or syphilis can cause disease, blindness or deformity in the foetus. The foetus can become infected as it passes along the mother's infected vagina during birth.

  AIDS can be passed from an infected mother to the foetus.

- **Diet**   This is an important consideration during pregnancy to ensure a healthy, well-developed child. Undernourishment or malnutrition (poor choice of diet) during pregnancy can result in the foetus being starved of the nutrients it needs. Extra calcium and Vitamin D are needed for strong teeth and bones, and iron and folic acid are needed to prevent anaemia. A varied, balanced diet, remembering the dietary goals of less salt, less sugar, less fats, more fibre, will result in a healthy, but not overweight, baby.

  Undernourishment, in very severe causes, will result in the death of the foetus. Less drastic undernourishment could lead to a very underweight baby with underdeveloped individual organs.

- **Poor antenatal care and ignorance of the risks**   These factors can result in foetal abnormalities of all kinds, simply because the expectant mother has not taken the necessary care of herself and her child during pregnancy. If she does not attend an antenatal clinic, the doctors will not be aware of any damage to the foetus, which could perhaps have been avoided.

Factors beyond the mother's control

- **Viral infections**   The most well known is German measles (rubella) which can severely damage the foetus, causing blindness, deafness or physical deformity. This can largely be avoided if all girls are vaccinated against the disease, and women who are pregnant or planning a pregnancy should check their immunity. As 50 per cent of foetuses are affected if the expectant mother develops German measles in the first three months of pregnancy, it is essential that she gets expert help in this situation. Other viral infections which may cause abnormalities are influenza, mumps, chicken pox and viral meningitis.

Cytomegalovirus is a virus infection of the cervix which can infect the foetus, causing jaundice, anaemia, blindness, or low birth weight. Toxoplasmosis is a disease usually caught from cats or from eating infected meats. If it is caught by the foetus from the infected mother it can result in encephalitis or hydrocephalus.

- **Rhesus incompatability**   This condition happens when a Rhesus negative woman has a Rhesus positive partner and the baby has Rhesus positive blood. The mother's blood reacts against the babies blood and may cause the baby to suffer from anaemia, jaundice or a weak heart. Good antenatal testing will detect this condition and steps can be taken to correct it.

- **Accidents**   Once the foetus is well established in the womb, it is well protected and can survive bumps, bangs and the mother falling. A severe accident, fall or shock towards the end of the pregnancy can cause the onset of labour with the possibility of an underweight baby. A sharp, direct blow to the abdomen could damage the foetus, but is very rare.

The expectant mother can help to prevent accidents by avoiding wearing the type of clothing and shoes that could increase the risk of falling (such as very long skirts or high heels), and by being conscious of her increased size and weight and her changing centre of balance. She should, as far as possible, avoid situations where accidents are more likely to occur, such as going into crowded shops.

- **Environment**   The expectant mother may live in a very unhealthy environment, but cannot necessarily move to a healthier one just because she is expecting a child. In heavily populated areas, the air may be polluted by factory fumes and by lead from petrol fumes; food may be contaminated by the heavy use of insecticides or by harmful bacteria; the ground may be contaminated by the faeces of animals; and water is sometimes polluted by factory waste, untreated sewage, or lead from lead water pipes.

Pollution can affect the expectant mother and her foetus, causing general physical or mental disorders. By being aware of these dangers the expectant mother may be able to avoid some of them. Strict rules of personal and food hygiene, fresh air whenever possible and exercise, will decrease these risks.

Complications at birth

Some abnormalities of the foetus exist at birth. Some of these are brought about because the baby is pre-term, or of low birth weight; some are diagnosed in the early postnatal stages. The earlier an abnormality can be diagnosed the earlier treatment can begin, and this may lessen the risk of the condition becoming severe.

Several standard tests are carried out on the newborn for early diagnosis of the more common complaints. These tests include:

- **the Agpar score.** This involves measuring the heart rate, breathing rate, state of the muscles, colour of the skin and response to stimulation. The higher the score out of ten (two marks for each of the five areas) the better the condition of the baby. A low score indicates that further treatment is needed. The test is done one minute after birth and repeated at five minutes after birth.

- examination for **cystic fibrosis** (see p. 96). If there is reason to believe the child may have cystic fibrosis, because a brother or sister has, or because a genetic test on the parents has shown that one of them carries the gene for cystic fibrosis, a sweat test and a blood test can be done some days or weeks after birth.

- **checking the hips** to ensure there is no dislocation.

- **checking the heart** for defects.

- **checking the head and spine** for conditions such as hydrocephalus, spina bifida, Down's syndrome, etc. Many of these conditions cannot be confirmed until the baby is several months old.

- **checking for cleft palate and club foot.**

- **the Guthrie test.** This is a blood test to check for PKU, and is reliable after the first week of life. The test is also used to check for thyroid deficiency.

There is a higher risk of damage to the foetus if there are any complications during labour, such as:

- a long, difficult labour.

- a large baby delivered by a woman with a small pelvic area.

- a pre-term or low birth weight baby.

- a breech birth – the baby arrives feet or bottom first.

- malposition – the baby is lying in a transverse position in the womb.

- foetal distress – the baby is showing signs of distress and needs to be delivered quickly.

- multiple births – the babies may be born prematurely, and the second baby to arrive is often weaker than the first.

The greatest risk during birth is that the foetus may become starved of oxygen, and this may happen in any of the circumstances given above, if the oxygen supply is cut off temporarily or the supply is reduced. This may occur because of a poor birth position, or if the placenta is not working well, or the umbilical cord becomes knotted or tightens round the baby's neck; or sometimes the newborn baby has respiratory problems and has difficulty with initial breathing. Lack of oxygen will damage the brain. Minimal brain damage may only show itself as clumsiness, lower intelligence, lack of co-ordination, or a minor physical defect such as having the pupil of one eye larger than the other, but the more severe cases of brain damage may result in cerebral palsy, epilepsy, and mental handicap.

Many physical or mental abnormalities can be avoided, or the effects reduced, if the mother and baby receive expert attention during the perinatal (delivery and birth) and postnatal periods. Early diagnosis and treatment of these conditions is then possible.

Childhood illnesses and infections

Even the healthiest of children will suffer from some of the illnesses and infections common to childhood. Most of these can be quickly cleared up, with the use of antibiotics if needed, but occasionally a very persistent infection, or one which has been neglected, can cause a permanent disability. The effects of infectious disease are usually quite mild, especially if the child has been vaccinated and has formed some resistance to the disease, but sometimes a particularly virulent strain of the disease occurs, giving a severe attack and leaving permanent damage.

Illness or infection which can leave permanent damage	Possible permanent effects
Respiratory infections, coughs, breathing difficulties	Asthmatic attacks
Rheumatic fever, tonsillitis, scarlet fever – all caused by streptococcus	Chorea, damage to the heart, ear infections, deafness
Bronchitis and pneumonia	Chest weakness
Meningitis	Partial or total deafness, convulsions (fits)
Measles, roseola	Middle ear infection, convulsions
Whooping cough (pertussis)	Kills nearly half of all infants under four months who are affected; can leave chronic lung disease, ear infections, retarded development. (In very rare cases the vaccine may cause brain damage and convulsions.)
Mumps	Meningitis, encephalitis
Poliomyelitis	Muscular paralysis

A variety of different physical reactions can also be caused by emotional stress. The most common are asthma attacks, hay fever, and infantile eczema (although these complaints have other causes as well).

Some serious conditions develop in the early years of childhood. Four of the most serious ones are cystic fibrosis, muscular dystrophy, leukaemia and spina bifida. Some of these conditions are irreversible and there is so far no cure for them, but a lot of research is going into their causes and treatment. The life of the child can be prolonged in most cases by skilled medical treatment.

- **Cystic fibrosis** affects about 1 in 2000 children. It is a condition which affects the lungs and digestive system, so that the child is unable to produce the digestive juices properly and there is an overproduction of mucus in the lungs. The child must have a special diet, treatment with antibiotics, and physiotherapy. The condition can be quite mild in some children and with good medical treatment many reach adulthood.

- **Muscular dystrophy** is an inherited disease in which the muscles gradually waste away. The commonest form is Duchenne, which affects boys under the age of five (although other forms affect girls too). About 1 boy in 10 000 is affected. There is no known treatment although physiotherapy can help. Boys with this condition often die before the mid-twenties.

- **Leukaemia** is a cancer of the white cells in the blood, leading eventually to excessive bleeding, fevers and pains in the limbs. Approximately 1 in 25 000 children are diagnosed as having leukaemia. Medical research has advanced so well that some strains of the disease can be cured, and many others can be treated so that the child's life is extended. The cause of the disease is unknown but radiation may be a contributor, which is why the expectant mother should avoid X-rays if possible.

- **Spina bifida** is quite a common congenital abnormality, which affects about 5 in every 2000 births. The child is born with some of the bones of the spine not properly joined together. Some cases are more severe than others, and surgery can often help to correct the fault. Severely affected children may be paralysed and many spina bifida children are mentally retarded.

Accidental injury

Unfortunately, large numbers of children are killed or injured accidentally every year, despite the publicity given by the accident prevention bodies. The charts opposite help to give an idea of the huge numbers of cases involved.

In many of these cases the accidents could have been avoided. Accidents are usually caused in part by: carelessness or not thinking ahead; inadequate supervision; ignorance; lack of common sense or of safety awareness; or forgetfulness. Accidents – inside and outside the home – are the major cause of death and injury to children aged 1–14 years.

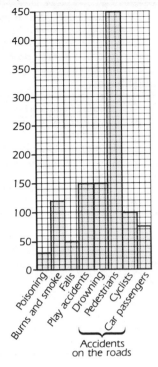

Deaths a year
(approx.)

450
400
350
300
250
200
150
100
50
0

Poisoning
Burns and smoke
Falls
Play accidents
Drowning
Pedestrians
Cyclists
Car passengers

Accidents
on the roads

Type of accident

Accidents per year resulting in death to children

Source: *ROSPA*

Injuries a year in
thousands (approx.)

160
140
120
100
80
60
40
20
0

Scalds
Poisoning
Glass cuts
Burns and smoke
Falls
Pedestrians
Cyclists
Car passengers

Accidents
on the roads

Type of accident

Accidents per year resulting in non-fatal injury to children (Play accidents result in large numbers of minor injuries.)

Source: *ROSPA*

Accidents in the home

Below and on the next page is a list of types of accident and their possible results.

Accident type	Possible long-term effect
Falls	*Can leave permanent physical and/or mental damage, such as paralysis, broken limbs which do not heal correctly, broken nose, teeth knocked out, scars to face and body, internal damage to chest and abdomen, skull fractures*
Burns and scalds (caused by unguarded fires, carelessly placed kettles, etc.)	*Can leave permanent scarring, hair loss, disfigurement, mouth burns; inhaling gas and fumes can lead to respiratory problems*

continued

Accident type	Possible long-term effect
Poisons	*Drinking insecticides, bleaches, and other corrosive liquids will damage the mouth and stomach; lead poisoning can cause anaemia, convulsions, kidney damage, brain damage; poisonous plants can cause death or severe damage*
Cuts *(from sharp knives, instruments, machinery, etc.)*	*Can result in severed limbs, fingers, etc.; permanent scars left from stitches; damage to eyes and ears* *Children are at particular risk from large glass patio doors which they may run into or push toys into*
Permanent loud noise	*Damaged hearing*
Flickering lights	*Flickering lights can bring on epileptic attacks*
Poor lighting	*Can weaken the eyesight*
Unsafe toys	*Can poison or cut, or damage eyes, ears, and nose*
Water in garden ponds	*May lead to asphyxiation – if breathing stops the lack of oxygen to the brain can leave permanent brain damage*

Causes of accidents in the home

Accidents outside the home

On the roads, the children most at risk are those who:

- have some form of physical or mental disability.
- come from families where there is insufficient care and road safety is not taught.
- have just come from other countries and may not be familiar with road problems in Britain.

The environment is also important. Children are at risk if they live in an area where there is a high density of housing, shops and work places, a lot of traffic, and few or no play areas. Children who live in the country, however, may be in danger from unlit streets and roads, country roads without pavements, farm machinery, and a lack of pedestrian crossings and other safe ways of crossing roads. When there is little traffic children are not so aware of its dangers and may take risks.

Accidents in the home, or on the roads may leave little or no physical effect but they can cause permanent psychological damage such as trauma, phobias and fears which last for the rest of the child's life.

It is often easier for a child and her family to accept the fact that she has a physical or mental handicap because of a congenital abnormality, than to have to recognise that a permanent handicap caused by an accident could have been avoided with a little more care and common sense.

Non-accidental injury

Non-accidental injury to children is done deliberately, often in the home; it is sometimes known as 'baby-battering'. It is difficult to know how common this is because only the more dramatic cases become well known. Many thousands of cases are dealt with by the local authorities and voluntary agencies, and it is certain that many more cases go unreported and undetected.

Some horrific examples of child abuse result in the death of the child, but many others leave children permanently disfigured or disabled, or emotionally scarred, because of the cruelty of the adults who look after them.

Types of child abuse

Some cruelty is *positive* – when an adult deliberately sets out to hurt the child and inflicts injuries such as:

- bruises on the face, and body, as the result of smacking, thumping or hitting with an object.
- bites to the body, which show as bruises or wounds.
- fractured and broken bones caused by throwing or pushing the child, or blows to the face which fracture the nose, jaw or skull.
- severe shaking of the child, which can result in multiple damage such as broken or fractured bones, severe bruising, and brain damage.

- burns and scalds. Sometimes a child may be put in a scalding hot bath, or burnt with cigarettes.
- poisoning. The child may deliberately be given drugs or poisonous substances.

Some cruelty is *negative* – when an adult deliberately neglects a child by:
- not feeding the child.
- not providing sufficient warm clothing or bedding.
- not keeping the child clean, thereby allowing infections, sores, nappy rash, scabies, and head and body lice, to occur and develop.
- neglecting the child when he is ill, thus allowing illnesses to become severe and leave permanent damage.
- leaving the child alone for long periods, causing emotional damage, loneliness, fears and phobias, and reduced chances for language and intellectual development.

Another developing area of cruelty is *sexual abuse*, when a child is subjected to sexual practices by an adult. There are over 1500 reported cases a year, and many more which go unreported. In 80 per cent of cases the child is female, and usually the adult is a young male, often a member of the family, and most often the father or father figure.

It is often difficult to identify cases of child abuse, as children may themselves take it as a matter of course, or be too afraid or too loyal to their family to report the matter to anyone. People who deal with children, such as health visitors, child clinic officials, social workers, teachers, and playgroup leaders, need to be aware of the danger signs which may indicate child cruelty. These include children having obvious unexplained injuries, such as frequent evidence of bruising, burns etc.; being dirty, hungry, or undernourished; being very quiet, retarded, and sullen; or being very aggressive and bullying. These signs may not indicate abuse, or they may indicate minor, temporary neglect, but they should always be checked.

Neighbours can also be a good source of information. It is *not* being nosey or unneighbourly to report the case of a persistently crying or screaming child, or adults who frequently hit or shout at their children. A confidential report to the police, the National Society for the Prevention of Cruelty to Children (NSPCC), or other officials, may save a child from horrific injury.

Causes

Child abuse can occur in any layer of society. It is not confined to families in poor circumstances with low incomes or living in bad conditions, or to families of low intelligence. There are, however, certain factors which put some children at risk. These include:

- parents who are under considerable stress because of marital difficulties, financial problems, unemployment, etc.
- parents of low ability, who are unaware of the needs of young children.

- parents who are too young, and do not want the responsibilities of family life.
- families where there are a large number of children, when some may be physically neglected, ignored or picked on.
- families living in very poor housing conditions, including overcrowding, isolation in high rise flats, inadequate sanitation and services, etc.
- parents who were themselves subjected to abuse as children, and often take it out on their own children.
- parents who are naturally bullies, sexually perverted, or inadequate in some way (for example, drug addicts and alcoholics), and use their children to relieve their feelings.
- parents of a handicapped child who may find the strain too much and may abuse the child.

Families in any of these circumstances are at risk, and once they are identified by the social or voluntary services they will be given special observation and support.

Most parents at some time feel frustrated and angry with their children, especially if they have had a series of sleepless nights or a period of stress. Some parents may be afraid that they may not be able to control their feelings and that they will harm the child. If the situation becomes this desperate they should seek advice. They should never stand by and allow a partner to abuse the child and do nothing about it. In many circumstances the authorities realise that cases of child abuse are the result of desperation, and they will try to help the family rather than simply remove the child.

Dealing with child abuse

Cases of child abuse are dealt with in several ways. The case may be taken to court and a care order awarded. The child is then under the care of the local authority until the age of 18. The parents cannot regain custody unless the care order is removed. Alternatively a supervision order may be imposed, under which the child can be returned home but the parents must accept supervision from social workers for a period of up to three years. The family problems can be investigated by social workers, and the welfare services co-ordinated to help to re-educate or readjust the family. The child can be removed from the risk, permanently if necessary, but usually as a temporary measure. If and when the child is returned to the home, constant support and supervision can be provided for the child and family to prevent any further abuse.

It is better to try to *prevent* child abuse rather than have to treat it when it has happened. Preventative measures include:

- encouraging the natural process of bonding which occurs between parents and child when the child is first born, and during the formative years.
- a good standard of education in child-bearing and child rearing, in schools and at antenatal and postnatal sessions.

- information easily available to parents on how and where to get help, through, for example, educational programmes on radio and TV.
- improvements in social, economic and environmental conditions, so that young families are not constantly struggling to survive.
- methods of detecting families at risk at an early stage so that they may be counselled and helped.
- cheap and easily available methods of family planning, so that couples can choose the size of family they want.
- the provision of daytime care such as day nurseries, mother and toddler groups, playgroups, and nursery schools, for children at risk, so that the parents have a few hours' break from the stresses of caring for the child.
- support for the voluntary societies which specialise in dealing with child abuse, such as the NSPCC, the National Children's Home, Dr Barnardo's, the Church of England Children's Society, and Parents Anonymous. Parents Anonymous is a voluntary organisation set up in 1976 to help parents who feel they are unable to cope and may injure their children. It is staffed by volunteers who will befriend the family, visit them and give help and support.

The child abuse syndrome is usually brought about by inadequate, desperate parents with social problems, rather than cruel uncaring parents who deliberately injure their children, but in both cases the result can be a permanently damaged child.

Diet and environment

Diet

Diet is an important factor in the health of every child.

Some children are born with a medical condition which makes them unable to tolerate or utilise some essential nutrients.

Some children, however, are fed too much of certain nutrients and not enough of others and will therefore suffer from *malnutrition*, while others are overfed and will therefore suffer from *obesity*.

Others again, especially those in some of the third world countries, do not get sufficient of any food and will suffer *starvation*.

Medical conditions
Examples of inadequate utilisation of food, and food intolerance conditions, include:

- **diabetes**   This is a condition in which the body is unable to convert sugar and starch into energy, because the pancreas does not produce enough of the hormone insulin, which is needed to remove excess glucose from the blood stream. The condition may be inherited, but details of the causes of diabetes are unknown. It can be controlled by diet and measured insulin injections.

- **coeliac disease or gluten sensitivity**   This means that the child is allergic to the protein part of most cereals and grain. When mixed feeding starts at about 4–6 months, cereals are introduced to the baby which he is unable to tolerate and absorb. This will result in lack of nourishment, failure to thrive, bouts of diarrhoea, anaemia and general irritability. It affects about 1 in 2000 people and the condition responds to the child being given a gluten-free diet.

- **PKU**   This is a condition in which the body is unable to metabolise phenylalanine, an amino acid which then accumulates in the body and can affect the brain, so causing mental handicap. The Guthrie test (see p. 94) helps to identify the disease and the child is put on a special low phenylalanine diet. It affects about one in 10 000–15 000 babies.

- **cystic fibrosis**   The pancreas does not produce sufficient digestive enzymes and therefore complete digestion and absorption of fat and protein is affected. The child therefore fails to thrive and may have persistent chest and breathing problems, which may eventually be fatal. The child will need to take a replacement pancreatic substance before each meal and may need to be put on a special diet.

- **lactose intolerance**   A few babies are unable to utilise the lactose in milk because they do not have enough of the digestive enzyme lactase. The result is a watery diarrhoea, tummy pains and a failure to thrive. If a lactose-free milk is substituted recovery should be quick.

- **milk protein intolerance**   Some babies are allergic to the protein in cow's milk, and this will be shown by such symptoms as failure to thrive, eczema, diarrhoea, vomiting, coughs and wheezing. The child may be able to tolerate goat's milk, but if not, a suitable plant milk containing soya bean protein should be substituted. (Goat's milk should not be given to a child under six months old.)

Malnutrition and obesity

A poor diet which does not contain the correct balance of nutrients can produce a child who is permanently unhealthy, with the possibility of severe dietary deficiency diseases, and/or the problems of obesity.

Fat

Too much fat in the diet will help to produce a fat person. Fat is used to produce energy, but if we do not burn off the calories which fat produces the result will be obesity. Obesity in a child results in the unsightly appearance of double chins, flabby arms and thighs and bulging chest and abdomen, and a slowness in becoming mobile. As the child becomes older, there will be increased risks of respiratory diseases, heart, lung and kidney diseases, high blood pressure, diabetes and varicose veins.

There are two main types of fat – **saturated** and **polyunsaturated** fats. Saturated fats are mainly from animal sources such as butter, cream, eggs, cheese and especially fatty meat; polyunsaturated fats are mainly of vegetable origin, such as vegetable oils, cereals, seeds and nuts. The saturated fats can cause a build-up of fat in the arteries, eventually leading to heart disease.

Therefore the two *rules* must be:

- Do not include too much fatty food in the diet.

- Use foods with a polyunsaturated fat content rather than a saturated fat content.

Sugar and starch

Too much sugar and starch (carbohydrates) in the diet will also provide unwanted calories and will produce an overweight child. In Britain, on average, each person eats about 50 kg of sugar each year, half of it in the form of sugar added to home-made foods and drinks such as tea and coffee, and half contained in the manufactured foods we buy. Even a can of baked beans contains sugar!

Sugar is almost totally pure carbohydrate, with no other nutritive value. A small bar of chocolate will provide 150 calories per 25 g, sugar provides 112 calories per 25 g, and one doughnut will provide 190 calories. Unless these calories are burnt off in activity, they will turn to body fat.

Another danger associated with too much sugar in the diet is the risk of tooth decay. The plaque (sticky film) which forms on the teeth all the time is largely made up of bacteria. When something sweet is eaten, it only takes about 20 minutes for the sugar combined with the plaque bacteria to produce acid, which attacks the enamel covering the teeth. Constant eating and drinking of sweet foods and liquids, especially if the teeth are not thoroughly and regularly cleaned, will lead to tooth decay.

Foods such as bread, cereals, potatoes, pastries and cakes contain a lot of starch and are rich in carbohydrate. They are needed to provide energy and bulk in the diet. As they are a comparatively cheap form of food they are often eaten in excess, and the excess is laid down in the body as fat.

Therefore the *rules* must be:

- Do not develop a sweet tooth in early childhood.

- Cut down on sweet, starchy foods such as cakes, biscuits and confectionery.

- Use sweeteners other than sugar, such as dried fruits and fresh fruit juices. Cut down the sugar content in cakes and give flavour with spices such as nutmeg and cinnamon.

- Read the labels on commercial foods, and avoid the ones which contain a high proportion of sugar and starch.

- Do not buy heavily sweetened squash and ice lollies – have fresh fruit drinks instead.

- As many medicines for children are sweetened with sugar, parents should request non-sweetened medicines.

Salt

Too much salt in the diet can eventually lead to high blood pressure in those people who are susceptible to it. We all need salt in our daily diet, but many people have much more than they require. One teaspoonful per day will cover our requirements, unless the body is losing salt through excessive sweating in hot weather or during heavy physical exercise. Salt, like sugar, is habit-forming and it can be difficult to cut down on it. It is best not to let a child establish a liking for salt.

Therefore the *rules* must be:
- When buying commercially prepared baby foods, look for the ones which have reduced salt content or are salt-free.
- Avoid commercially prepared foods with a high salt content such as smoked haddock, kippers, tomato ketchup, and yeast extract. Many food labels state the amount of salt contained in the product.
- Do not put the salt pot on the dining table – just put the required amount in during cooking.
- Reduce or miss out the salt in many cooked dishes and use alternative flavourings such as herbs, spices, lemon juice, garlic, pepper, etc.
- Do not give salted peanuts and crisps as snacks. Use fresh fruit or vegetables or dried fruit instead. After a while the taste buds will become accustomed to the less salty flavours.

Additives

Most of the processed foods which we buy contain food additives, which are chemical or natural products used to preserve and colour the food, and to enhance and give flavour. Many of these additives are harmless, and the preservatives are necessary to prevent the food deteriorating. Some of the colourings, flavourings and enhancers in current use may not have been thoroughly tested, however, and it is believed that if they are taken in excessive amounts they can cause conditions such as hypertension, hyperactivity, skin rashes and general debility, and asthmatic or breathing difficulties. Parents and child carers should therefore be prepared to use fresh, wholesome foods as much as possible, using convenience foods very sparingly. Careful reading and understanding of food labels is essential.

Breakfast Cereal

for babies from 4 months

SUGAR FREE

JUNIOR FOOD
Chicken Dinner

Milupa Junior Foods taste so good because we use only high quality, natural ingredients. The special recipes include small, tender pieces to encourage your baby to learn to chew and to enjoy different textures. Milupa Junior Foods are easy to prepare – simply mix the contents of this sachet with hot, previously boiled water to required consistency. Stir gently to allow pieces to soften.

- Soft pieces to encourage chewing
- Nutritious, tasty meals
- No preservatives, no artificial colourings or flavourings
- Milk free
- Also good for the elderly and convalescent
- Gluten free

Ingredients:
Rice, maltodextrin, chicken, soya flour, dried vegetables (peas, cauliflower, potato, leek, green beans, onion, carrot, savory, parsley), vegetable fat, oleo oil, cornflour, meat extract, vitamin concentrate (containing vitamins C, E, Ca-D-pantothenate, nicotinamide, vitamins B_1, A, B_2, B_6, folic acid, biotin, vitamins D_3, and B_{12}), calcium carbonate, spice, iron (as ferric pyrophosphate).

Typical analysis per 100 g:
Protein 12.9 g. Fat 9.3 g. Carbohydrate 72.3 g.
Vitamins:
Vitamin A 330 µg (retinol equivalent), B_1 1.3 mg. B_2 0.28 g, B_6 0.24 mg, B_{12} 0.47 µg, Biotin 6.8 µg, Ca-D-pantothenate 2.6 mg, Folic acid 47 µg, Nicotinamide 2.6 mg. Vitamin C 28 mg, D_3 (cholecalciferol) 4.8 µg. E 3.3 mg.
Minerals:
Calcium 0.2 g. Sodium 0.3 g. Iron 5 mg.
Energy:
approx. per 100 g 425 kcal = 1793 kJ.
These analytical values are subject to slight variations normally accepted with natural products.

Labels showing the contents of commercially prepared foods

Deficiencies

Having not enough of certain nutrients will also cause illness and disease. Vitamins, minerals and fibre are essential in our diet and insufficient of the foods which contain these nutrients will lead first of all to poor resistance to infections; poor quality of skin, hair, teeth, and nails; restricted development; constipation and digestive problems; and a generally low standard of health. More acute conditions are likely to result eventually in a vitamin or mineral deficiency disease which can leave permanent damage. The table that follows shows some of these results.

Nutrient	Found in	Importance to the body	Deficiency results
Vitamin A	*Milk, dairy products, green vegetables, liver, margarine, fish liver oil*	*Helps fight infection, needed for healthy skin and normal growth*	*Skin disorders, poor resistance to disease, disturbed vision*
The B Vitamins	*Cereals, meat, fish, eggs, milk, yeast extract*	*Helps to utilise food, needed for nervous system* *Cannot be stored for long in the body*	*Slow growth and development, diseases such as beri beri*

continued

Nutrient	Found in	Importance to the body	Deficiency results
Vitamin C (Ascorbic acid)	Fresh fruits and vegetables, blackcurrant and rosehip syrup	To fight infections, for teeth and bones, good skin and blood vessels Easily destroyed by cooking, cannot be stored in the body	Poor resistance, retarded growth, scurvy
Vitamin D	Margarine, butter, milk, fish oil, some breakfast cereals Also obtained from sunlight	Needed to help the body absorb calcium for strong bones and teeth	Dental decay, rickets
Calcium and phosphorus	Milk, cheese, green vegetables, fish, hard drinking water	Needed in the formation of bones and teeth, blood clotting, muscle function	Decalcification of the bones, poor teeth, excessive bleeding
Iron	Liver, red meat, eggs, green vegetables, oatmeal, dried fruit	Formation of the red blood cells which transport oxygen round the body to release energy	Anaemia
Sodium and chlorine	Found in common salt	Maintain water balance and muscular functioning	Severe cramp
Iodine	Sea fish, shell fish, iodised table salt	Functioning of the thyroid gland	Goitre

Fibre

Fibre is essential in the diet, but the refined diets of the Western World usually only provide half to three-quarters of the amount we require. We need fibre in our diet to act as roughage which aids digestion. Fibre will:

- stimulate the activity of the intestine.

- help to prevent or relieve constipation, and encourage regular bowel movement.

- give a feeling of fulness by absorbing water, and so help to prevent overeating while contributing very few calories.

- help to reduce the absorption of fat.

Fibre may be **soluble** or **insoluble**. Soluble fibre is contained in fruits and vegetables, pulses (peas, beans and lentils) and oat, barley or rye products. It helps to restrict the amount of fat we absorb into our bodies. Insoluble fibre is contained in flour, bread, cereals, bran and some vegetables. It soaks up moisture and provides bulk in the digestive tract, which stimulates the elimination of waste products.

Children should be encouraged to include fibre in their diet. Insufficient fibre can lead to chronic constipation and digestive disorders.

Therefore the *rules* must be:

- give them wholemeal or high fibre bread, brown rice and wholemeal pasta.
- include plenty of fruit and vegetables in their diet, especially fruit and vegetables in their skins once the child can cope with them.
- give the child snacks of muesli bars and dried fruits, instead of refined sweets and biscuits.
- give plenty of breakfast cereals (not sugar-coated) which contain bran or oats, or have porridge for breakfast.
- sprinkle a spoonful of bran on to cereals, puddings, yoghurt, etc.
- use brown flour for baking cakes and pastries.

Environment

The environment in which a child lives can be an important contributory factor towards her state of health.

Air, land and water can be polluted, especially in areas of dense population. Bacteria in polluted surroundings can cause many types of disease or intensify a condition which a child already has.

Air can be polluted by fumes from traffic. These fumes contain lead which can build up in the body to a dangerous level and produce lead poisoning, a condition that can lead to anaemia, hyperactivity, lower intelligence levels and reduced ability. Modern paints are lead-free but many old houses still have old paint that contains lead; this can flake off and may be accidentally eaten by children.

Smoke, dust, pollen, and chemical waste from factories can all cause respiratory problems in children. The Clean Air Act (1956) restricts the amount of permitted waste from factories, and controls the type of fuels which householders can use.

Land which has been treated with chemical fertilisers or insecticides can pollute the food we eat, causing allergic reactions and intestinal problems. Animal faeces in parks, in grassland, on the street or on the beach may be handled by children who could then swallow worm eggs from the faeces. These eggs can cause a severe infestation (toxocariasis) which can lead to blindness, liver, lung or brain damage in the child.

Water can become polluted, especially in rivers, streams or some coastal areas, when factory waste or untreated sewage is pumped into the water. It is usually only when children are swimming or paddling in this type of water that there is a risk of infection. Polio is associated with polluted water in paddling pools or swimming baths which have been insufficiently treated with chlorine. Drinking water in the UK is normally very safe; the only dangers are if the water passes through old lead pipes (now being replaced by copper or plastic pipes) or contains a high concentration of nitrates. Nitrates occur naturally in the water, but during times of drought the concentration may become dangerous and a harmful blood condition (methaemoglobinaemia) may result, especially in young, bottle-fed babies.

These environmental diseases are quite rare and families who take normal hygiene and safety care should not be at risk.

It is clear that many of the physical or mental handicaps which children are born with, or develop during childhood, could be avoided or reduced in severity by:

- more concentrated medical research;
- greater access to genetic counselling;
- better antenatal and postnatal care, and care during birth;
- more use of preventative measures such as immunisation;
- a wider accident prevention and first aid educational programme;
- greater surveillance on children at risk in problem families;
- diet and nutritional education available to all; and
- government and community provisions for a healthy environment.

8 The Handicapped Child in the Family

What are the special needs of the handicapped child and the child's family? Children with a physical or mental handicap have the same basic needs as any other child. They require:

- adequate shelter, warmth, clothing, sensible diet, rest, exercise and hygiene.
- protection against infection and danger.
- opportunities to mix and communicate with other children and adults.
- materials and opportunities for play, to help with normal development.
- people who will teach them the basic skills needed to live in our society.
- caring loving parents or guardians who will provide a secure environment.

Because of their disability they may also have *special* needs, which may include:

- **special aids**   If the child has reduced mobility, is partially sighted, or has a hearing defect, etc., he may need special equipment such as a wheelchair, calipers, or a crawler trolley. He may need appropriately designed cutlery, cups, dishes and feeding aids; large type or Braille books; and specially designed toys.

- **house adaptation**   As the child grows older the house he lives in may need to be adapted to his needs. The doorways may need to be widened for a wheelchair, a downstairs toilet may be needed, handrails may be required in the toilet and bathroom, etc.

- **medical supervision**   The child may need supervision, treatment and/or hospitalisation for the rest of his life. It is important that his condition is monitored regularly, the relevant treatment given and any special drugs, diet or therapy are provided.

- **special education**   There are several options open for the handicapped child and the choice will depend upon the severity of his condition, the education facilities in his area, and his parents' wishes.

Small children very quickly adjust to their own handicap and the use of wheelchairs, hearing aids, insulin injections, and physical and mental therapy becomes a routine part of their lives. The important thing is that the child is treated as far as possible *just like any other child*. His parents, his family and relations, and the people he comes in contact with, must all treat him naturally; if he is good he must be rewarded, if he is naughty he must be punished, just as his brother or sister may be. This is a very difficult thing to do, especially by parents who may have been devastated by the shock of his handicap.

The parents

The reaction of parents when told that their baby or child has a handicap often follows a set pattern. At first, they may be unable to take in the full impact of the news and become numb with shock. After that, there is often a period of disbelief when they search round for alternatives, followed by feelings of anger that this has happened to them, and of guilt that maybe this has happened because of something they did. Finally these emotions settle down and usually there comes an acceptance of the situation. A few parents reject their handicapped babies as soon as they see them and can never bring themselves to accept the child. More often, though, usually they develop strong feelings of love and protection for the child, and then he can become overprotected and overpowered by his parents' desire to do everything for him. It is eventually easier, for instance, for the child with a severe facial disfigurement to get used to and accept the stares and whispers he is going to get, rather than be kept hidden away and overprotected by his parents.

The parents of the handicapped child need:

- full information at all times about the child's condition.
- expert advice and counselling from qualified and experienced medical and social workers.
- financial support when necessary.
- priority with rehousing or adapting present housing.
- day care for the child.
- opportunities for meeting other people at social events.
- mobility – help with transport for themselves and the child.
- short-stay residential care for the child to enable them to have a break.
- long-stay residential care if and when the child should ever need it.
- community support and understanding.

One of the major problems families of handicapped children may have is their isolation because of the indifference and lack of understanding shown by so many other people. Despite this, however, many parents and families cope very well with the care of their handicapped child. They are able to provide a relaxed, happy and loving atmosphere.

Provisions for help

Provisions are made by the government (statutory help), local authorities, and voluntary societies to help handicapped children and their families.

Throughout history the care of the handicapped has fallen upon families and neighbours, with some help from the Church and charitable institutions. It was not until the Poor Law Act (1601) that local government took some responsibility in providing for 'the sick, the needy and the homeless'.

During the eighteenth and nineteenth centuries, help for the disabled was inadequate and unevenly distributed, and it was not until the Education Act (1914) that special education had to be provided for epileptic and mentally handicapped children by the local authorities. In 1948, the National Health Service was introduced by Aneurin Bevan, and this set out to:

- meet the health needs and improve the physical and mental health of the people;
- cover all the needs of those who required it;
- provide free services, the expenditure to be financed from general taxation;
- give efficient and well-planned hospitals and services.

The NHS has contributed greatly to the improvement in the standard of health of the nation; improved the general health of children; increased life expectancy and reduced the infant mortality rate; and reduced the financial worries which illness and handicap bring.

Statutory help

The statutory help now available from the government and local authorities to help handicapped children and their families includes:

- **preventative measures** such as ante- and postnatal testing, immunisation programmes and medical research to try to identify and eliminate the causes of handicap.
- **free medical care** under the NHS, including free prescriptions; free dental and optical services; free allocation of special aids; access to specialists and the required treatment; therapy (physio-, occupational and speech) and hospitalisation when necessary.
- **specialist health visitors and medical social workers** who are specially trained to keep in contact with the child and his family and give advice and support.
- **development centres** (in some areas) where a team of medical and social workers give treatment to the child and all-round family care.
- **free milk and vitamin drops** up to the age of 5 years and from 5 to 16 years if they are not getting them at school – given according to family income.
- **care groups** such as day nurseries, playgroups, mother and toddler groups, opportunity groups, and nursery classes (available in most areas), some of them specially organised for handicapped children. Priority must be given to the handicapped child if the group is run and funded by the local authority.
- **home helps**, child minders, and laundry facilities (only sometimes available).

- **housing.** Most local housing authorities will give priority to families with a handicapped child and either provide a bungalow or ground floor flat, or adapt the house they live in, or allocate an improvement grant for bathroom and toilet facilities.

- **leisure facilities** such as special play areas, riding facilities, swimming tuition, social clubs and other pursuits, either specifically for handicapped children or where they can mix with other children (only sometimes available).

- **special holiday homes** or foster parents where handicapped children can go for a short holiday to give their family a break (some local authorities only).

- **finance.** This is perhaps the most important need of the family with a handicapped child. He may require special care; special diet, accommodation, clothing, toys, and transport; and full-time supervision. All this will be a financial drain to the family. Government provisions available include:

  - normal child benefit for which *every* child is eligible, income support, family premium, family credit (*see* Section D), as applicable, and possibly:

  - attendance allowance for children over two years who need constant looking after because they are severely disabled. There is a lower rate for day *or* night attendance, and a higher rate for day *and* night attendance.

  - mobility allowance for children over five years unable to get about unaided. This is a weekly allowance to help parents with taxi fares and/or car allowance to transport the child.

  - fares or petrol costs for visits to hospital, either to take the child for treatment or to visit the child.

  - free transport to school or day-centre.

  - possibly a clothing, heating or food allowance for the child for families on low incomes.

  - a supervisor, free of charge, for children who need to travel between home and a residential hospital or school.

There are additional possible finances for severely handicapped children. If the child has become severely disabled as a result of vaccination, he may be eligible for a lump sum vaccine damage payment. A fund set up by the government and directed by the Joseph Rowntree Memorial Trust, the Family Fund, helps to provide things for the severely handicapped child which are not covered by the grants listed above. It may award money, but usually it provides equipment, clothing, bedding, or holidays which the child would not normally get.

Although all these facilities should be available to all handicapped children and their families, some local authorities are better at providing them than others. It is up to parents to pressurise their local council to make the provisions available for all.

Advice about what the child is entitled to, and how and from where to get the benefits, can be obtained from the Citizens' Advice Bureau; the child clinic and health clinic; the GP, health visitor, or social worker; leaflets from the public library or post office; the social services department; or the social security office. DHSS leaflets should be filled in and sent to the address given on the leaflet.

Education

By law, the local authorities must provide education for all children according to their needs. This is especially important for the handicapped child, who will need to begin a learning programme when he is very young. He will need specialised teaching to make the most of the abilities which he has, and to develop those of his senses which are impaired.

The very young child is best looked after in his own home. His parents are his best educators, with the help of an **advisory teacher** who will visit the home and advise on a learning programme. The child must be taught self-help skills from an early age so that he can eventually take his place in the community.

Special schools which cater for the needs of children who are deaf, blind, disabled, slow learners, etc., often have nursery classes for 3–5-year-olds to start their training. Home teaching is available for children too severely disabled to attend a school. Some local authorities provide **family centres**, where families with handicapped children can meet for discussion and use the facilities offered, such as toy libraries, reference books, information from voluntary societies, social security information, etc.

There are three main ways of educating handicapped children:
- special residential schools;
- special day schools; and
- special units attached to ordinary schools.

In the past most handicapped children used to be sent away to a *special residential school*, sometimes as early as $2\frac{1}{2}$–3 years of age. The feeling was that these children needed to start being trained while still young, and training needed the skills of special staff. The disadvantages of this type of education are the trauma experienced by the child and the parents at the early and frequent partings, and the loss of contact with the home for several weeks at a time. Children tend to become institutionalised and isolated in their own small world of handicap, and parents are not greatly involved with the child's upbringing. It is also costly to the taxpayer to set up and maintain residential centres.

Special day schools are better then residental care because they overcome most of the problems listed above. As there are relatively few children needing special education, however, there is only a need for a small number of special schools, and often the handicapped child may face a very long daily journey to get to the nearest one appropriate to his needs.

Learning and playing at RNIB's Rushton Hall School

Recent years have seen the development of the *special units* plan. Many ordinary schools now have a special unit where ESN (educationally subnormal), visually handicapped, hearing impaired or mobility handicapped children can be given special teaching, but can also join in with the social life and perhaps some of the activities of the school. Where the degree of handicap allows, handicapped children can receive some or all of their lessons in ordinary school classes, if necessary accompanied by their own assistant. In this way handicapped children become accepted by other children and are not isolated in a handicapped group. (These units are not suitable for the child with a severe form of handicap.)

Children's hospitals must provide a hospital teacher for those children who have to spend long periods in hospital. Most special schools liaise with further education establishments, and these days many handicapped children continue into colleges or universities in the same way as other children would.

Voluntary help

Although the state provides a great deal of help for the handicapped and their families, there are still many services which need to be covered by the volunteer groups. There are thousands of volunteer groups which are mainly occupied in:

● giving general information about cash allowances, housing and other amenities available for the handicapped.

- campaigning for better conditions, better treatment and better recognition in the community.

- raising money for specific projects such as holiday homes, specialised equipment, treatment for individual cases and research projects.

- bringing together 'handicapped families' for discussion and social meetings.

- organising playgroups, youth clubs, outings, and leisure activities for handicapped children.

- co-ordinating individual voluntary workers and putting them in touch with those who need help.

- forming a link with the statutory services to ensure that the families obtain maximum benefits.

Most voluntary agencies are run as charitable organisations and are funded by public donations and collections. Some have varying amounts of aid from the government or local authority. Most of them are unable to give cash handouts, although they sometimes provide clothing, special equipment or toys; but their most useful function is to give information, advice and support to the handicapped and their families. Voluntary work is of great value to the community and the statutory services would be much more difficult and expensive to run without the help of the voluntary organisations and voluntary workers.

These are examples of just a few of the voluntary organisations, loosely grouped into the types of work they mainly do.

General help
The following organisations give general help to the handicapped and their families:

Citizens' Advice Bureau

National Marriage Guidance Council

National Children's Home

Dr Barnardo's

Shelter

National Campaign for the Homeless

Parents Anonymous (telephone answering service for parents who have become desperate and cannot cope)

National Association for the Welfare of Children in Hospital

Child Poverty Action Group

Voluntary Council for Handicapped Children

Disabled Living Foundation (provides information and literature on all aspects of disability and provides the details of all the organisations which deal with specific handicaps)

Community Health Councils (help users of the NHS; there is one located in every district health authority)

Specific handicaps

The following are examples of organisations that can give detailed information about the handicap they specialise in dealing with. They are often a source of literature, aids, holidays, social events, fund raising campaigns, research campaigns and information relating to that particular disability.

MENCAP (Royal Society for Mentally Handicapped Children and Adults; offers all types of information and support to parents of mentally handicapped children)

Association for Spina Bifida and Hydrocephalus

Multiple Sclerosis Society

Down's Children's Association

National Deaf Children's Society

British Epilepsy Association

Royal National Institute for the Blind (RNIB)

Self-help groups

There are many organisations which are formed as self-help groups, or pressure groups, or as social groups for families to help each other. These include:

Contact a Family with a Handicapped Child (puts families in touch with each other)

Meet-a-Mum Association (practical help on a mother-to-mother basis)

National Deaf–Blind Helpers' League

Association of Parents of Vaccine Damaged Children.

CLEAR (campaign for lead free air)

Association of Carers (helps those whose lives may be restricted because they are looking after a disabled child or adult)

Prospect (campaigns for parents' rights on the treatment of handicapped children)

Hyperactive Children's Support Group

Talking Books and Magazines for the Blind

Voluntary service

A large number of individuals from all age groups and all walks of life do some form of voluntary service work. This can be:

● reading to the blind;
● playing with children in hospitals;
● assisting with physiotherapy programmes in the home of a handicapped child;
● assisting with and organising playgroups and youth clubs for the handicapped;
● helping with classes in swimming, riding, dance, etc.;

117

- assisting with speech therapy and communication;
- taking out wheelchair-bound patients;
- making things to sell and raising money for handicapped children.

The National Council for Voluntary Organisations helps to co-ordinate voluntary activities and organise volunteer centres in many towns, where individuals can offer their skills to help others.

Effects on the family

Having a handicapped child or children is bound to affect the rest of the family. It is often assumed that the effects on the family will be negative, but some very positive results can also be brought about.

Negative effects

The parents may be so severely disturbed by having a handicapped child that they develop physical and/or emotional problems and are unable to cope. There is a higher incidence of marital problems in families where there is a handicapped child.

Friends and relations may be embarrassed by the child and therefore keep away from the family, or may resent the handicapped child and try to blame the parents and criticise their actions. This increases the tendency for the family to become isolated, because most of the family's energies and resources are directed into coping with the handicapped child. The mother and/or father may be unable to keep a steady job because of the demands of the handicapped child.

There may be a financial drain because the child needs special equipment, food, etc., and the rest of the family may have to go without. Other children in the family may be deprived of outings and holidays because there is not sufficient money, or because the handicapped child cannot go. They may resent the amount of time their parents have to spend with their handicapped brother or sister. They may also be neglected or have to do much more for themselves than is normal, and they may be embarrassed and hurt by the teasing and unkindness of their school friends.

Positive effects

Family bonds may be strengthened, as the mutual problems and decisions to be made can draw parents closer together. Close links may be established with relations and friends who are willing to help. The other children in the family often develop a deep love for their handicapped brother or sister and enjoy helping with or playing with him or her; and they can develop a strong sense of responsibility and general feelings of sympathy, compassion and understanding for the handicapped.

The family's social life can be improved and extended through contact with the relevant voluntary groups, and taking part in organised outings and holidays with families in similar circumstances.

Play for handicapped children

A handicapped child, like any other, will learn through play. The child may develop much more slowly than most children, or may be slow in some areas of development but very quick in others. He may appear to make good progress sometimes and little progress at other times. Much will depend upon the severity of his condition, but there are very few conditions where play activities cannot be of benefit.

Activities, games and toys must be planned to:

- suit the child's condition and requirements;
- develop the skills he is good at and improve the areas where he has difficulty;
- suit his mental stage of development – not necessarily his age;
- give him training in life skills so that he will become as independent as possible;
- involve him with other children, some handicapped like himself, some not;
- let him mix with other adults so that some of the pressure can be taken from his own family;
- give him constant rewards and encouragement which help him to persevere with his efforts; and
- challenge him to make further efforts.

All play activities should be fun and give enjoyment. As soon as it becomes a struggle or the child is bored or frustrated, the activity should be changed.

The handicapped child should be given opportunities for:

- **physical activity** This develops muscular co-ordination, confidence and independence.

- **intellectual development** The mentally retarded or brain-damaged child will progress at a slower rate and need simple activities, but there will be a gradual build-up of knowledge and experiences.

- **imaginative and creative play** The child can get a lot of satisfaction from producing a picture or a model or a tune, and may be better in this area than his non-handicapped companions.

- **social play** This gives the child the pleasure of being with others, learning to give and take and preparing for adult socialisation.

119

Activities and toys for the physically disabled child
Physical activity

General physical disabilities
The following will all help to develop balance and co-ordination:

baby walker, baby's first car, push-along toys, building bricks, rocking horse, skittles, tricycle, scooter, hammer and peg toy, climbing frame, rope ladder, and swings.

For the more seriously impaired there are toys such as a play shell (a safe, fibreglass rocking shell), a moulded go-cart, a walk-along car or scooter boards.

For hand and arm co-ordination
Suitable toys include modelling clay, bead threading, jigsaws with large pieces, battery toys, easy-grip action balls, bean bags, and water play toys. Activities such as horse riding, swimming and ball games will help with co-ordination and balance.

For hearing impaired and autistic
Useful toys include electronic games, activity centres, telephones, puppets and a toy theatre. Bubble blowing, balloons and sound puzzleboxes will help with speech therapy and breath control.

For the visually handicapped
Suitable toys include musical toys, ball with a bell inside, raised letter blocks, large beads and building blocks, and toy typewriters. Fitting shapes into holes is a useful activity.

Imaginative and creative play

Imaginative play
The child should be allowed to fantasise and pretend – this is a natural stage of development. Dressing up costumes, bought or made dolls, soft toys, action man, doctor and nurses sets, masks, and face paints, are all good for this.

Creative play
Materials for creative play may include paints, crayons, play-do, jumbo crayons, plasticine, water, sand, gardening equipment, fabrics, paper, old magazines for cutting up and making collages, old boxes, cardboard cylinders, plastic bottles, etc. These can all be used for 'bits and pieces' toys.

Intellectual development

Numeracy and literacy skills
Number- and picture-matching games, lotto, dominoes, card games such as snap, picture trays, pegboards, clocks, scales, measuring jugs, baking sets, and magnetic and electronic educational games, can all help.

Discriminating shape, colour and size
There are many teaching programmes specially developed for the needs of handicapped children. Stacking boxes, posting box, card matching, sound lotto, floor puzzles, and ludo are useful.

Social play

Play which imitates adult roles
'Mothers and fathers', tea parties, a
Wendy house, and play shops, will
train the child for adult life.

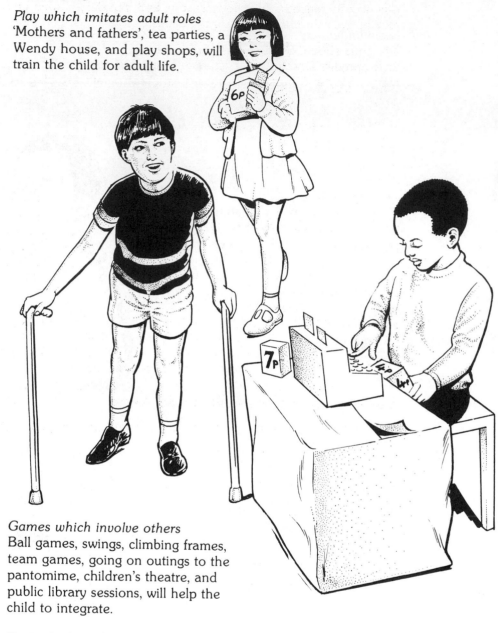

Games which involve others
Ball games, swings, climbing frames,
team games, going on outings to the
pantomime, children's theatre, and
public library sessions, will help the
child to integrate.

Toys which help develop social skills
Practice jackets give practice at
buttoning up, zips, press studs, and
buckles. Imitation shoes help with
shoe fastening. Special toothbrushes,
shaped soap, well-designed cutlery
and dishes help with hygiene and
table skills.

The important things about toys and activities for the handicapped are that they should teach in an enjoyable way, and that they should be *safe* and allow for the special requirements of the child.

Before you buy ask yourself these questions:

- Will it splinter?
- Is it strongly made?
- Has it any sharp edges?
- Has it any sharp pieces sticking out?
- Is it non-toxic?
- Could a child swallow any of the pieces?

Specially designed toys can be very expensive, but the child should not be given a toy he cannot use, as it will only frustrate him. It is possible to adapt some ordinary toys for use by handicapped children; perhaps the toy can be mounted on a strong board, small knobs can be replaced by larger ones, seats can be padded or adjusted. Many parents of handicapped children make toys themselves. Ideas and patterns can be obtained from special books and from the sources shown below.

Some of the large-scale toys such as the Playshell, the Totally Soft Play Environment or the Transporter Trolley are too expensive or too large for the normal household, but are often part of the equipment of the special playgroup, child development clinics or special schools.

Sources of information and help

Help in choosing and using special toys for the handicapped is obtainable from:

- the health visitor;
- the therapist who works with the child;
- the psychologist;
- the playgroup or day nursery;
- the local clinic;
- the child development centre;
- the social services department; and
- the society or voluntary group relating to the child's needs.

Toy libraries are a very good source of information and help for specialised needs. They are run by voluntary organisations to provide toys and equipment for children who need them. Toys are put on display and a child may choose one to take home to play with for a short time. The toys are checked, repaired and cleaned regularly. ACTIVE is part of the Toy Libraries Association which deals with the needs of the handicapped by producing aids for communication, teaching, leisure and play. They produce work sheets to help parents make suitable toys for their handicapped child.

Other useful organisations and publications

Directory for the Disabled – available from the public library

National Association for the Welfare of Children in Hospital, Exton Street, London SE1 8UE – provides leaflets on play for children in hospital

National Children's Bureau (NCB), 8 Wakely St, Islington, London EV1V 7QE

National Council for Voluntary Organisations, 26 Bedford Square, London WC1B 3HU

National Toy Libraries Association (NTLA), 68 Churchway, London NW1 1LT

Play Matters – part of the NTLA; publish many useful books and leaflets including *Good Toy Guide* and *Easy-to-make Toys for your Handicapped Child*

Community support

The effects of having a handicapped child in the family are far-reaching. It has been estimated that the cost of raising a child without a handicap is about £70 000 (figures from the Legal and General Insurance Company). For the family with a handicapped child the *extra* ongoing costs and loss of earnings of carers could amount to £62 750 (figures from the Disablement Income Group).

As well as financial problems, there is the emotional distress and the strain put upon a marriage when a handicapped child requires constant care.

The community must make sure that these families receive as much help and support as possible, by:

- providing adequate financial help and suitable housing.
- making medical treatment and assessment procedures available for the child.
- providing therapy and training programmes for the child.
- updating existing services and providing new amenities.
- providing leisure activities and companionship for the children and their families.
- educating young people to accept and help the handicapped.
- putting national resources into research which will eventually reduce the incidence of handicap.

The passage that follows helps to sum up the requirements of children with handicaps and their families. The handicapped child's needs are the same as those of any other child – a happy, stable home, a loving family, good physical care, friendship and companionship outside the family circle, and the support of the community. The move towards integrating children with handicaps into the community is a good one, and playgroups, schools and social groups all benefit from the inclusion, while it improves the quality of life for families with problems.

Case history: A day with David

The mother of David, who was born without legs and with tiny arms, describes a typical day (drawn from fact).

I start my day at 6.45, usually feeling tired and depressed. David was born sixteen years ago and it has been a constant struggle to care for him and the rest of the family. My husband died some years ago and my other children left home early because they could not stand the pressures of life with a severely handicapped brother.

It is hard work caring for David. He is very heavy to lift and when I am dressing him we often fall over, have a good laugh and start again. He can eat his own food, using the digits on his tiny arms very well. He is a bright, placid boy, very affectionate and with a sense of humour. He is intelligent and is doing very well at the local comprehensive school he attends.

I have to do everything for David, such as washing him completely at least twice a day, comb his hair, take him to the toilet, change his clothes, etc. I get tired and depressed but he is more resilient than me and has no hang ups about being handicapped. He is always telling me not to worry but I cannot help it. I resent the embarrassment felt by other people and our loneliness and isolation. Sometimes my next door neighbour will help but my family have not bothered about us for years.

We watch TV in the evenings and David does his homework. I wash and change him ready for bed and eventually go to bed myself. It takes me a long time to get to sleep despite my long, hard day. I worry about the future but decide that it's best to take things a day at a time.

Summary and Evaluation

Quite a lot of children are in need of special care. It may be that they have a physical, mental or emotional handicap, or they may come from a socially deprived background, all of which makes them feel different from the other children they play with or go to school with. Because of pressure from other people, children hate to feel different – they like to look similar to their friends and to come from a similar home and family background. Anything which makes them feel different, such as a handicap, or coming from a broken family, being part of a family with a criminal background, or living in poverty, can upset them and they may resort to behaviour such as:

- becoming aggressive, antisocial and attention-seeking.
- being withdrawn and unable to make social contact.
- telling lies to conceal their family situation.
- developing problems such as bed-wetting, stuttering, petty theft, etc.

If parents, carers, teachers, social workers, etc. can identify children with these problems as early as possible, deal with the cause, and give sympathetic help and support with specialist treatment when necessary, the children's quality of life will improve and they will not grow into the type of insecure, inadequate adults who pass on the shortcomings of their childhoods to their own children.

Fortunately, most children are robust and adaptable and manage to cope with their own difficulties and family circumstances very well. They usually love their parents or carers, and if they receive even a small amount of affection in return they will manage to survive the rigours of poverty, neglect, abuse or in some other way feeling different.

For those children and their families who cannot cope so well with their problems a great deal of help is available, from that given by friends and neighbours to the statutory financial and social benefits provided through the DHSS. These, plus the extensive range of voluntary help that exists, ensure that most families with special needs have somewhere to go for help and advice.

Follow-up Work

Fact finding exercises

1   Suggest six possible causes which could result in a child being handicapped from birth.

2   Describe four tests carried out on the newborn baby which are used to detect chronic (long lasting) handicaps

3   The information in the following table has been mixed up. Match each of the conditions with a possible cause.

Condition	Possible cause
Deafness/blindness	Smoking or drinking alcohol during pregnancy
Child with below average intelligence	Use of strong drugs during pregnancy
Stunted growth	German measles during pregnancy
Physical deformity	Dietary deficiency during pregnancy

4   Explain the meaning and give some examples of:
    a)   sensory handicaps (that is, those that affect the five senses); and
    b)   interrelated handicaps.

5   What do you consider to be the main *general* causes of accidents in the home?

6   Which of the following do you think is the nearest to the approximate number of accidental injuries in the home to children per year?
    26 000   300 000   1 000 000   150 000

7   What is the difference between malnutrition and starvation?

8   Suggest some alternative flavourings to replace salt and sugar when cooking or serving these dishes:

Salt	*Sugar*
chicken casserole	stewed fruit
green vegetables	rice pudding
savoury rice	muesli bar
mashed potatoes	fruit squash

127

Data response and problem solving exercises

1

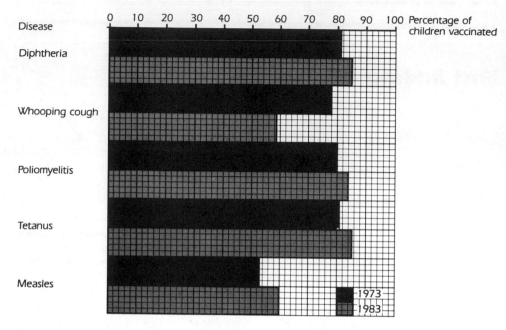

Vaccination and immunisation of children in Britain, 1973 and 1983

Source: *Social Trends 1985*

a) Does this chart show a general increase or decrease in the numbers of children vaccinated in 1983?

b) Find out

  i) why there has been such a dramatic drop in the proportion of babies being vaccinated against whooping cough.

  ii) why the numbers of cases of whooping cough in 1978 and 1982 were very high.

2 What signs would lead you to believe that a small child was being ill-treated, and what would you do about it?

3 Which of the foods in this list are high in fibre?

wholemeal bread	cheese	eggs
apples	baked beans	white bread
baked custard	frozen peas	dried apricots
ricicles	butter	breakfast bran
prunes	porridge	jacket potatoes

Select some of the foods in this list to plan a midday family meal which is high in fibre and low in salt, sugar and fat content.

4 Why is it so important for handicapped and normal children to mix, and what opportunities are there for this?

5

Divided dish with suction lid – the base can be filled with hot water

Non-slip table mat

Two-handled mug

Spoon and fork with thick handles

Brush or comb with extended handle

Describe how these pieces of equipment could help a handicapped child.

6 From the list below, select some things which would be of special value to:

a) a visually handicapped child.

b) a mentally retarded child.

c) a child with impaired hearing.

Give reasons for your choice.

balloons	toy typewriter	finger paints
tape recorder	mirror	drum
telephone	thick-grip crayons	large wooden beads
talking books	ball with a bell in	activity centre

Free response questions

1 Compare the risks of environmental pollution in the inner city areas with those in the countryside.

2 Compare the advantages of educating a physically handicapped child in a residential school with those of allowing the child to attend a special unit attached to a normal school near home.

3   Explain why children living in these family circumstances may be at risk.

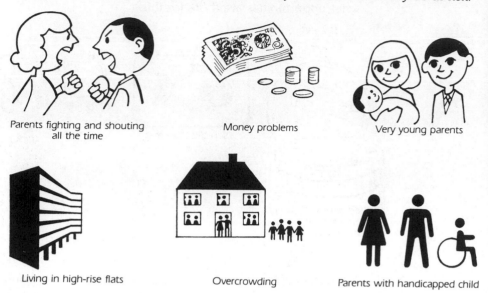

Parents fighting and shouting all the time

Money problems

Very young parents

Living in high-rise flats

Overcrowding

Parents with handicapped child

4   Write an essay about *either*

The voluntary work which I do to help the handicapped

or

The ways in which young people can help the handicapped.

Activities

1   *a)*   Make a teaching book for a visually handicapped child, using large letters, brightly coloured pictures, raised numbers, and textured objects.

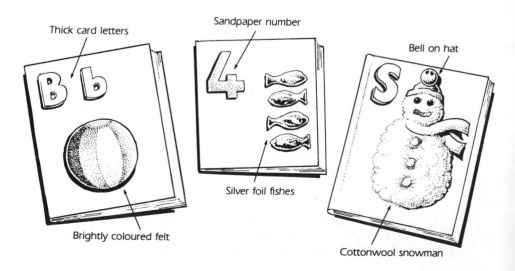

Thick card letters

Sandpaper number

Bell on hat

Brightly coloured felt

Silver foil fishes

Cottonwool snowman

b)   Make a toy from fabric or wood which would help a child with poor muscular co-ordination.

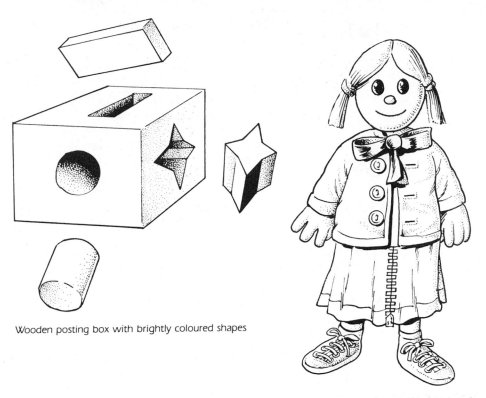

Wooden posting box with brightly coloured shapes

Rag doll with buttons to fasten, velcro strips, zips, bows and shoe laces

2   Discover what special facilities there are in your town or village for handicapped children.

Make a booklet which could be given to the parents of handicapped children in your area, containing information about:

mother and toddler groups/playgroups; local branches of voluntary societies; cinemas, theatres, restaurants, leisure activities; baby-sitting services; where special aids may be bought or borrowed; and anything else which could be of value to the handicapped.

SECTION D Community Care and Provision

9 The Welfare State

There have always been families in this country who, because of their inability to obtain sufficient food, clothing and shelter, have lived in poverty. Throughout history, these people were helped by the Church, by rich people and by their own friends, neighbours and families. Until the beginning of the twentieth century, government and voluntary assistance was limited to helping paupers and the most seriously disadvantaged. From then on, the State slowly extended its help to other aspects of the community, covering unemployment, poor housing, health, medical services, education, etc. After the Second World War, the idea of the Welfare State emerged, with the **Beveridge Report (1942)**. This report advised the setting up of welfare services to reduce 'want, disease, squalor, ignorance and illness', and so help to eliminate poverty. The aim was for the State to give assistance to every citizen who needed it 'from the cradle to the grave'.

Over the next few years, many Acts of Parliament were passed on the basis of the Beveridge Report to provide the basis of our welfare services as we know them today. Examples are:

- *Family Allowance Act (1945)* – payment of 5 shillings (25p) per week for each child after the first, up to school leaving age.
- *National Insurance Acts (1946)* – financial entitlements for sickness, unemployment, retirement, industrial injuries, maternity grant and allowances, etc.
- *National Health Service Act (1946)* – all health services free of charge.
- *National Assistance Act (1948)* – established the National Assistance Board which gave assistance to those not covered by insurance.

In 1966 the Ministry of Social Security was established to be responsible for social services, and in 1968 the Ministry of Social Security and the Ministry of Health were amalgamated to form the Department of Health and Social Security (DHSS). The DHSS was responsible for:

- social security payments, which provide cash benefits for those in need.
- the National Health Service (NHS), which covers personal and mental health and environmental health.
- the welfare of the elderly; of the physically and mentally handicapped; of children; of the homeless; and of special groups such as immigrants.
- education, including preschool, adult and special education.
- employment opportunities and services such as retraining people or transferring people from one job to another.

- housing, including provision of accommodation and town and country planning.

The early Acts passed by the government have been developed and changed, although much of the principle remains. For example:

- The family allowance was gradually phased out, and replaced by the *Child Benefit Act (1975)* which gives a tax-free payment for every child up to school leaving age.
- *The Family Income Supplements Act (1970)* introduced the family income supplement (FIS) for families on low incomes.
- *The reorganisation of the NHS in 1974* brought about many changes in management, use of resources and patient care.

All these provisions must of course be paid for, and the money for welfare services comes from general taxation and National Insurance contributions. Approximately 13.2 per cent of the national budget in 1983 was spent on social security programmes, and approximately 12.5 per cent on health services.

In 1988 the DHSS was again split into two departments:

- the Department of Social Services (DSS);
- the National Health Service (NHS).

Social security rights and benefits

Some State benefits are available for everyone whatever their income. Some are only for those who have paid the required amount of National Insurance contributions, and some are only for those on low incomes. Because there are so many State benefits, the system can be very confusing, and it is usually best to get help and advice. Help can be obtained from:

- the local social security office (DSS);
- the social services department of the local council;
- the DSS Freephone – dial 0800 666555;
- the Citizens' Advice Bureau; and
- DSS leaflets covering all individual benefits, available from DSS Leaflets Unit, P.O. Box 21, Stanmore, Middlesex, HAZ 1AY. Health visitors and social workers will also advise.

Source: *Leaving School?*

Sources of help and advice

Place	Help given	Listed in telephone book under
Careers office	*Advice on jobs, training, etc.*	*Careers service, or the name of your local education authority*
Citizens' Advice Bureau	*Anything*	*Citizens' Advice Bureau*
Employment Office/ Jobcentre	*Advice on jobs, training, etc.*	*Employment Services Division*
Housing department	*Advice on rents and rates*	*Your county, district or London borough council*
Local education authority	*Grants for school and other students*	*Your county, district or London borough council*
Tax office or PAYE enquiry office	*Advice on tax*	*Inland revenue*
Social security office	*NI leaflets, claim forms for social security benefits*	*Health and Social Security*
Unemployment benefit office	*Unemployment benefit, credits*	*Employment*
Students Union	*Financial, welfare advice*	*College at which you are a student*

Source: *Leaving School?*

The social security system is in a state of change. After considerable research, the government decided on a massive overhaul of the system, and the Social Security Act (1986) was introduced with the aims of:

- simplifying the social security system.
- giving help to those who most need it – for example, low income families with children, the disabled, and the chronically sick.
- removing the old system with its many different types of benefit, which could lead to unfairness and confusion.
- removing the situation in which it was financially better to remain unemployed than to work – known as the 'poverty trap'.
- modernising the system and making it more efficient.

It will take several years to bring about all the proposed changes, and although a timetable has been planned, this is subject to delays and alterations. According to the proposed timetable:

- uprating of benefits (increasing them once a year in line with the cost of living) will take place in April as from 1987. Upratings used to take place in November.

- some changes were made in April 1987, including statutory maternity allowance and new arrangements for help with maternity and funeral costs.
- all reforms to be in place by April 1988.

The present reforms and those which are planned include the ones in the following sections.

Reforms

The supplementary benefit system ended in 1988, and all income-related benefits are now calculated in the same way whether a person is employed or unemployed.

Income support replaced supplementary benefits. It is made up of:

- *personal benefits* – a basic personal allowance, family premium, family credits, and child allowances.
- *housing benefit* – those on the same income, whether working or not, will receive the same benefits, and the maximum payments will be 100 per cent of rent and 80 per cent of rates.
- a *social fund*, to provide maternity grants, funeral grants, and interest-free loans.

Benefits for parents and young children

- *Child benefit*   This will continue and will be paid to the mother. It will be tax free and will increase as the child gets older.
- *Family premiums*   Families on income support will be entitled to a flat rate sum and benefits such as free school meals, free milk, etc.
- *Family credit*   This will replace family income supplement and will be paid in the paypacket. It will be available for people who have children and work 24 hours a week or more. Low income families will get cash help instead of free school meals and welfare milk.
- *Income support*   This will be given to disabled children and adults .There will be an extra family premium for a child with a disability.

In assessing the income-related benefits, the first £5 earned by a person will be disregarded – £15 for lone parents, long-term sick parents, and parents unemployed for over two years.

Maternity benefits

The maternity grant (£25) was abolished in April 1987. Those on low incomes and in receipt of income support can be eligible for a maternity grant from the social fund. The maternity allowance will be replaced by statutory maternity pay (SMP). It will be payable by the woman's employer for up to 18 weeks if she has been in that employment for at least 26 weeks. Women will have more choice when to give up work, but it must be at least six weeks before the baby is due.

137

Supplementary benefit and family income supplement were gradually phased out as the new schemes took over.

Other benefits available

DSS benefits
● *A dot in the column means that that benefit is available for that category.*

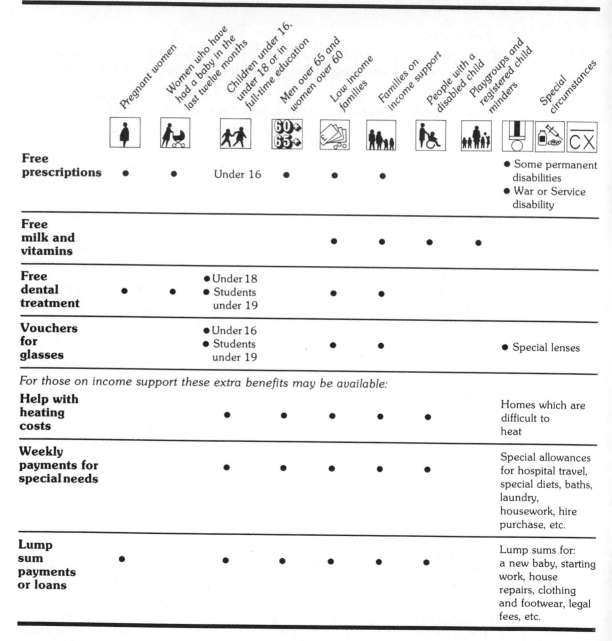

	Pregnant women	Women who have had a baby in the last twelve months	Children under 16, under 18 or in full-time education	Men over 65 and women over 60	Low income families	Families on income support	People with a disabled child	Playgroups and registered child minders	Special circumstances
Free prescriptions	●	●	Under 16	●	●	●			● Some permanent disabilities ● War or Service disability
Free milk and vitamins					●	●	●	●	
Free dental treatment	●	●	● Under 18 ● Students under 19		●	●			
Vouchers for glasses			● Under 16 ● Students under 19		●	●			● Special lenses

For those on income support these extra benefits may be available:

	Pregnant women	Women who have had a baby in the last twelve months	Children under 16, under 18 or in full-time education	Men over 65 and women over 60	Low income families	Families on income support	People with a disabled child	Playgroups and registered child minders	Special circumstances
Help with heating costs			●	●	●	●	●		Homes which are difficult to heat
Weekly payments for special needs			●	●	●	●	●		Special allowances for hospital travel, special diets, baths, laundry, housework, hire purchase, etc.
Lump sum payments or loans	●		●	●	●	●	●		Lump sums for: a new baby, starting work, house repairs, clothing and footwear, legal fees, etc.

Further details about these and other benefits will be found in the relevant leaflets.

To claim social security benefits:

- the post office or social security office will have the necessary claim form and prepaid envelope. They will help the claimant to fill the form in if necessary.
- the CAB, local health clinic, and public library usually keep some claim forms or will advise people how to get them.
- sometimes there are claim forms attached to the relevant leaflets, which can be filled in and sent to the DSS. Examples are shown below.

Benefits are paid by Giro cheque (cashable at a post office) for lump sums, or by a book of weekly orders to be cashed at the post office on a certain day, usually within three months of the date on it. The benefits for certain items such as clothing, furniture, spectacles, etc., are paid by voucher.

Despite the social security system, some people do still live in poverty and it can be a very bleak existence living on state benefits.

Child Poverty Action Group postcard

Some facts

- In 1948 one person in 33 was dependent on supplementary benefit. In August 1983 the proportion was 1 in 8.
- The number of families with children who claim supplementary benefit has more than doubled since 1979, to 1 057 000 in 1986.
- The national average household spending in 1986 was £162 per week; some families of four in 1986 lived on a supplementary benefit of £59.05 a week.
- Many children who get into trouble, or who are taken into care, come from a deprived home background.
- A considerable number of people do not collect the benefits to which they are entitled because they do not know about them, are unable to fill in the claim forms, or are too proud to claim.

The National Health Service

Ideas for the setting up of a national health service were being suggested from the beginning of the twentieth century, but it was not until 1948 that the NHS came into existence, after the Minister of Health, Aneurin Bevan, had brought into force the National Health Service Act passed in 1946.

The broad aims of the NHS were:

- to meet all health needs and improve physical and mental health;
- to make all services free of charge;
- to meet all expenditure from general taxation;
- to make all services, including hospitals, efficient and well planned;
- to offer freedom, by patient and doctor, to join the service; freedom for patients to choose their doctors and dentists; freedom for doctors and dentists to remain in private practice.

The NHS immediately became very popular and was regarded with envy by other countries. The scheme was and still is very successful. There has been a general improvement in the nation's health, infant mortality rates have dropped, and there is greater life expectancy. Babies now have a twelve times better chance of living beyond their first birthday than in the early years of Queen Victoria's reign: babies died in their first year of life in 1983 at a rate of 10.2 in every 1000, compared with 148 in every 1000 in the 1840s. The death rate was cut from 21.4 of every 1000 people in the 1840s to 11.8 in 1983.

The scheme has led to a better distribution of doctors, hospitals and health services, and to the removal of financial worry when a person is ill. However, as the system progressed it was found that it was costing a great deal of money and was not very cost-effective. Resources were being wasted because of poor management and cumbersome structure.

Organisation

In 1974, the NHS was reorganised to make it into an integrated service. It is now run at three operational levels, **regional**, **area**, and **district**, under the overall control of the Department of Health and Social Security.

- *Regional Health Authorities*   There are fourteen of these, responsible for administration, finance, building, employment, and guidance.
- *Area Health Authorities*   There are ninety of these, responsible for assessing the needs of their own area, and for planning health provisions and organising the health services for that area.
- *District Management Teams*   These are responsible for the organising and management of the hospitals, clinics, health centres, home nursing, health visitors, doctors, and facilities for the elderly and handicapped in their district. There are usually about two or three districts per Area Health Authority.

All regional and district health authorities have general managers who are responsible for short- and long-term planning.

General criticisms

The NHS has gone through many changes since its beginning, mainly due to changes of government policy, recessions, financial difficulties, and staff and patient dissatisfaction. Charges or part payment have been introduced for prescriptions, spectacles and dentistry. (These charges are not made for people on low incomes.) There are long waiting lists for some treatments, especially those considered non-urgent. A number of hospitals and small units have been closed because they were not cost-effective, and some specialists have moved abroad because of dissatisfaction with salary, prospects and working conditions. The service is abused by some people because it is free and they waste doctors' time and resources.

Despite these difficulties, the NHS provides a reasonably efficient service, available to all at a very low cost.

Services
NHS services include:

- **maternity care** – pre-conception care and advice; family planning centres; infertility treatment; genetic advice and treatment; routine medical care during pregnancy; antenatal clinics; antenatal screening; specialists to deal with pregnancy problems; welfare milk; dietary supplements; ambulance service; hospital or home delivery; postnatal care; specialist care for difficult births; home visiting; routine postnatal checks.

- **services for babies and children** – postnatal tests; care of premature babies; advice on feeding; treatment and care of the handicapped; residential and day care for the severely handicapped; immunisation programme, baby and child health clinics; special services for visual and hearing problems; speech therapy; dentistry; psychiatric testing; psychological treatment; school medical programme which checks sight, hearing, teeth, and hygiene; general physical and mental developmental testing.

- **general services** – primary health care (the service provided by family doctors, dentists, opticians and pharmacists to give community care); ambulance and emergency services; hospital treatment, which includes intensive and long-term care, in-care, day care and out-patient treatment; convalescent and home nursing services; advanced technological treatments such as organ transplants, coronary bypass operations, hip and other joint replacements, and in vitro fertilisation procedures.

- **services for elderly people** – specialist medical care; residential or day care; walking aids; hearing aids; medical supplies; home treatments; bathing; chiropody; home helps and laundry services; special hospice establishments for the terminally ill (not just the elderly).

The emphasis is now on community involvement and support to allow the sick, handicapped and elderly to remain and be cared for in their own homes with only short-stay periods in hospitals or convalescent or residential homes.

The NHS also helps to finance and support *research work* into many ongoing problems such as heart disease, cancer research, effects of non-prescribed drugs, alcohol, smoking, AIDS, etc.; and *preventative* measures such as the anti-smoking and drugs misuse campaigns, healthier eating information, immunisation campaigns and advice, and cervical screening and breast examination to detect early stages of cancer or abnormalities.

The *Health Education Authority* (previously the Health Education Council) is funded by the DHSS and deals with all aspects of health care and preventative measures. It provides literature and educational material, organises displays and exhibitions, and gives lectures and educational talks on all aspects of health.

Staff
NHS professional staff and personnel include:

- general practitioners or family doctors. Patients may choose their own doctor. GPs deal with all aspects of health care and refer patients to hospitals and specialists when necessary.

- health visitors or community nurses, usually attached to a health centre. They are responsible for medical care at the centre, at child welfare clinics and in the home. They are Registered General Nurses (previously SRNs) with extra training.
- community midwives. They look after a woman during pregnancy and the birth and for 28 days after the birth.
- community psychiatric nurses, who look after patients in need of psychiatric help.
- consultants in obstetrics, gynaecology and geriatrics, who deal with cases needing specialised treatment.
- nurses specialised in mental illness and mental handicap.
- dentists, opticians, pharmacists, chiropodists, occupational therapists and physiotherapists.
- social workers attached to health centres, hospitals and clinics. They are able to deal with personal and social problems.

Some facts

	1978	1984
Family doctors	21 040	24 035
Family doctor list size	2 312	2 089
Dentists	11 919	14 334
Number of sight tests	7 800 000	9 700 000
Home helps and organisers	46 670	53 150
Hospital midwives	11 980	13 800
Psychiatric nurses	971	2 231

These figures show some of the improvements which have been carried out in the NHS over the years. We compare favourably with other countries, as is shown in the table below.

	Population per doctor	Number of doctors	Number of dentists	Number of midwives	Infant mortality rate (per thousand live births)	Expenditure on public health (% of national budget)
Austria	441	17 028	2 072	1 091	12.8	13.0
Costa Rica	1 502	1 600	448	—	17.3	5.1
France	516	104 073	30 321	9 382	9.3	15.0
Netherlands	498	28 807	6 271	974	8.3	11.7
Nigeria	9 591	8 037	285	27 983	140.5	2.4
UK	618	90 600	2 321*	21 663	11.0	12.8

*Government health employed personnel only

Figures are for 1980/81.
Source: *Britannica World Data*

Private health schemes

People who wish to do so may join a private health scheme such as BUPA or PPP, or they may pay independently for their health care. They may wish to do this because they believe they will get better facilities, better attention, quicker treatment and private facilities.

This may be true, but many people are against private medical care because they feel that it withdraws some resources, such as doctors, from the health service, and encourages two levels of health care. It gives an opportunity for some to jump the queue. Private care goes to financially well-off areas and many people believe the disribution of services therefore becomes uneven. Private patients do, however, pay twice – once in their National Insurance contributions and taxes, and once in their private health fees.

10   Voluntary Work

The work done by the DHSS is paid for by National Insurance contributions, taxes and money from prescriptions, etc., and the work is done by paid employees, but this work is given tremendous support by volunteer workers. There are many jobs in the social and health areas which do not need highly paid professional skills. Such things as shopping for the elderly, helping with handicapped children, or helping in hospital shops, provide valuable community service and can be done by unpaid volunteers. The country relies very heavily upon voluntary workers, and much more money and many more paid workers would be needed if people were not prepared to do voluntary work.

Voluntary work is done by:

- the individual worker doing jobs such as helping an elderly or handicapped neighbour, or giving transport to people going into hospital or helping at old people's clubs, etc.

- volunteers who are organised by a specific organisation such as the WRVS, the Samaritans, the Marriage Guidance Council, etc. Some of this work may require special courses of training and going through a selection procedure; Marriage Guidance, for example, requires quite lengthy training and not everyone is suitable for the job.

- volunteers who work for one of the thousands of charity organisations such as MENCAP, Oxfam, NCH, etc., and give active help to raise money for the charity.

Being a voluntary worker is open to every age group from the teenager to the elderly and can involve skills as wide as washing up, hairdressing or accountancy. It can also be very rewarding for the volunteers themselves, as people can forget their own minor problems when helping to look after people who are worse off than they are.

Investigation

As part of your examination work you could usefully carry out an investigation into voluntary work. It is a very extensive subject, so you could choose just one aspect to study, such as the historical background to voluntary work; voluntary help for the young family; volunteering to help the handicapped; voluntary community care for the elderly; or voluntary help for the teenager in trouble.

Answer some of these questions to help you with your project:

1 What would you consider to be the necessary characteristics of a good voluntary worker? Would it depend upon age, social class, education, religion?

2 List some of the points in favour of voluntary work and some of the disadvantages.

3 If you wanted to become a volunteer, how would you go about finding a job to suit your interests and capabilities?

4 Is it necessary for the volunteer to work closely with the paid professional, and if so, why?

5 What are the benefits to the volunteer of doing voluntary work?

6 Give some examples of voluntary organisations which require periods of training and special skills.

7 Describe some of the ways in which voluntary organisations raise money.

8 How do people who are in need of help get information about the voluntary aid available for them?

9 What are self-help groups? Are they a form of voluntary service?

10 Why does voluntary help need to be very well organised?

Summary and Evaluation

The United Kingdom is a very wealthy society and everyone living in this country is entitled to share in the country's wealth and expect a good standard of social services and health care. Wealth and resources are often unevenly distributed and sometimes those in need do not receive sufficient help, or those living in one part of the country receive more benefit than those in other areas. There will never be enough money to give everyone the standard of living or standard of health care which they would like, but reorganisation programmes, research, better planning, and increased efficiency can all help to make improvements.

It is in everyone's interests to see that parents and children are given the help and support which they need as they are our future, and it is only the most savage and inhuman cultures that do not care for their handicapped and elderly people.

Follow-up Work

Fact finding exercises

1 Explain the meaning of the following initials:

DSS   NHS   FIS   LA   NI   CAB   PO

2 Explain the following terms:

statutory benefits   integrated service
Freephone   dietary supplements
Giro cheque   private practice
primary health care

3 Which of the following people or places will help to sort out the social security benefits to which you are entitled?

public library   trading standards department
post office   CAB
social security office   health visitor
policeman   solicitor
environmental officer   Child Poverty Action Group

Problem solving exercises

1 Select suitable characteristics from the lists shown below to draw up four personality profiles suitable for performing the following voluntary work:

a) being on a busy Samaritan helpline.

b) fund-raising for Age Concern.

c) helping in a hostel for the homeless sponsored by Crisis at Christmas.

d) assisting at a playgroup for mentally retarded children.

Give reasons for your choice.

reliable	cautious	quiet
efficient	sensitive	adaptable
mid-twenties	generous	determined
intellectual	elderly	thrifty
modern	partially handicapped	traditional
self-confident	practical	imaginative
middle-aged	tolerant	extrovert
very active		

2 *a)*   Describe the statutory benefits available for people in the following situations:

  i) a single mother with two children under five years old, living in a rented flat.

  ii) parents with a severely crippled child needing 24-hour-a-day attention.

  iii) the wife and children of a man serving a long-term prison sentence.

b)   How will these families find out about the benefits they are entitled to?

c)   Which voluntary organisations could help these families?

Free response questions

1   Discuss the relationship between high unemployment and the high uptake of social security benefits.

2   Give some examples of the ways in which some people abuse the health services. How can pharmacists be of help with minor health problems?

3   The perinatal death rate for babies in social group 5 is almost double that of social group 1 (see socioeconomic groupings, p. 70). Indicate some reasons for this situation and suggest ways in which this problem can be tackled.

4   Assess the value of the reforms made to the social security system.

Why was it necessary to replan the old system?

What changes would you have introduced given the opportunity?

Activity

1   The average weekly household spending is £162 (including rent and rates of £32.50).

a)   Plan a weekly budget for an average family of four with this expenditure, and do a weekly budget for a family of four living on income support of £75 a week (not including rent and rates).

b)   Survey your local shops and consumer advice information centres to discover:

  i) Which is the cheapest form of fuel for heating and cooking?

  ii) Is it cheaper to buy food from a hypermarket, a supermarket, a chain store, a corner shop, or a market stall?

149

iii) Where do you get the best deal when purchasing furniture or large items of electrical equipment – a small specialist shop, high street multiples such as Curry's or Wigfalls, discount stores such as Comet, or catalogues or catalogue stores such as Littlewoods or Argos?

c) Summarise your findings. You could produce a booklet which would help money-conscious families.

APPENDIX A **Further Reading**

Useful books of reference, in addition to those suggested in Volume 1, include:

Introduction to Child Development Patricia Hicks (Longman)

Your Growing Child Dr Miriam Stoppard, Prof. Martin Herbert, Dr Geoffrey Ivimey (Octopus Books)

From Birth to Five Years Mary D. Sheridan (NFER–Nelson)

The Baby and Child Book Dr A. and Dr P. Stanway (Pan)

Social Services Made Simple A. Byrne, C. P. Padfield (W. H. Allen)

Lett's Study Aids: Home Economics

The Good Toy Guide compiled by Play Matters/The National Toy Libraries Association (A. C. Black)

A Handbook of Consumer Law compiled by the National Federation of Consumer Groups (Consumers' Association/Hodder and Stoughton)

Sources of statistical information include:

Encyclopaedia Britannica Year Book

Key Data '86 (Central Statistical Office)

Social Trends (HMSO)

Useful booklets, leaflets, etc. include:

Children Today and other publications (NCH)

National Welfare Benefits Handbook and other publications (CPAG)

Leaflets issued by the DSS

APPENDIX B Sample Examination Question and Marking Guidelines

The following question may help you to understand how some examination questions are planned. This is an example of a *structured* question – that is, it is divided into different parts. The question is also *stepped*: the first parts ask for simple recall of basic information; the following parts ask you to apply your knowledge; and the final part asks for an evaluation of the situation. The question therefore becomes increasingly difficult.

You can see by the mark allocation that only a small percentage of the marks are allocated to the first parts of the question. The bulk of the marks go to the more demanding aspects. So to obtain the maximum number of marks, always answer, as fully as you can, the latter parts of any question. If there is a choice of question, do not choose to do a question where you can only answer the first few parts. Plan your answer to the more demanding parts of the question carefully so that you do not become repetitive and wordy.

This question is based on a problem-solving approach and requires evidence of your own ideas and assessment of the situation and, where possible, any personal involvement or experience.

To obtain the most value from this exercise, answer the question first and then check your answer with the marking guidelines. How many marks do you think you would have obtained?

Sample examination question

Mrs Jones has a daughter aged 18 months, who does not seem to respond to sound. She suspects that the child may have a hearing defect.

		Marks
a)	Name *two* professional people to whom Mrs Jones could go for help.	(2)
b)	Give *three* medical causes for deafness.	(3)
c)	Briefly describe how and at what age (approximately) babies and preschool children are given hearing tests.	(4)
d)	Deafness affects speech development. Suggest *three* ways in which the hearing-impaired child can be encouraged and helped with communication skills.	(6)
e)	Assess and discuss the educational needs of children with hearing difficulties and the state educational provision which is available for them.	(10)

25

Marking guidelines

a) 1 mark for each of two suggestions: family doctor; health visitor; doctor or nurse at a child health clinic. (2)

b) 1 mark for each of three causes: pre-birth – a viral infection during pregnancy such as German measles, a genetic defect, the effect of drugs, brain damage; congenital malformation, severe jaundice when born; diseases and infections such as *otitis media* (infection of the middle ear), mumps, meningitis, encephalitis, blockage of the ear by wax or a foreign body; accidental or nonaccidental injury; repeated ear infections; damage to the auditory nerve. (3)

c) 4 marks for age and clear description of hearing tests: the startle reflex after birth may be regarded as the first test; routine medical tests after birth may indicate a defect but this cannot be accurate; between 7 and 8 months, all babies are tested for hearing at home or at a clinic, by a doctor or by a health visitor. Each ear is tested using distraction test – sounds are made at varying distances whilst another person distracts the child. His responses are noted. At 18 months–2 years more formal tests take place – co-operation testing. The child is asked to perform certain tasks connected with objects and his responses are noted. Further tests as required may be carried out at an ear, nose and throat department by audiologists. (4)

d) 2 marks for each of three ways suggested: very few children are totally deaf, as much use as possible must be made of any hearing ability; hearing aids can be used even by very small children, parents and adults can speak clearly and close to the child's ear, repeating sounds and words; therapy and exercises for the child to provide experience with the use of the lips, tongue, teeth, vocal chords – for example, blowing, sucking; feeling parent's or teacher's throat to recognise sound vibrations; lung and diaphragm exercises to teach air control; sign language and lip-reading may be taught as visual aids; playing games and using toys which encourage communication skills, such as play acting, miming, musical toys. (6)

e) 10 marks for two or three points relating to the child's educational needs and an informed description of the education options: the educational needs of the hearing-impaired child are the same as for a normal child, namely, opportunities for physical development, social contact, imaginative and creative work and intellectual development, but also taking the child's handicaps into consideration. Wherever possible, education should take place alongside normal children with additional special training and therapy given to help the child cope with the handicap. The child will need to be taught special communication skills such as lip-reading and how to make contact with 'normal' people. He may need psychological help.

State provision: residential schools with nursery departments, children kept until 16 or 18 years. Many of these are being closed as the feeling is to get these children into the community. Contact with parents is broken for long periods.

Special playgroups or nursery schools which accept children with a handicap.

Day schools for hearing-impaired children where children are bussed in from a wide area. Again these segregate the handicapped child and give him a long day away from home.

Small special units attached to normal schools: the child joins in with lessons such as craft classes, PE, etc., and has special tuition for his special needs. There is still a degree of segregation but the child feels he is treated more like a 'normal' child and so do the parents.

Children with hearing difficulties (unless very severe) can attend an ordinary school and have a special 'helper' who is trained to assist with their education, and care for their needs. (10)

APPENDIX C Suggestions for Practical Work and Investigations related to GCSE Techniques

The coursework which you will be asked to complete as part of an examination syllabus is very important. It will be allocated 40, 50 or 60 per cent of the total marks (the remaining marks being for theory papers) and will be school-based; that is, it will be awarded marks by your teacher(s) over the whole period of the examination course. This is called internal assessment.

The form of coursework required will be laid down in the syllabus of the examination board chosen by your school, but most boards require all or some of the following:

- a study of a child or group of children.
- one or more investigations into specific problems or situations which come within the syllabus. Some examination boards give specific topics for these each year.
- an item to be made by the candidate for use by a child. Some examination boards specify the item(s) to be made.

The aims of the GCSE examinations are towards 'pupil centred learning': this means the active involvement of the pupil. You should choose topics for your coursework which involve the skills of:

- problem solving and decision making;
- observation and enquiry;
- organisation and management of resources;
- manual dexterity and practical skills;
- understanding and explanation;
- planning and recording; and
- analysis and evaluation.

General points about coursework

1   The choice of a coursework topic is very important. It should be something which interests you and which is within your capabilities.

2   Do not keep starting new projects and leaving them because you get bored.

3   Your order of work should be: planning – execution – evaluation: all are equally important.

4 Your teacher may help you with selecting a topic by offering some suggestions, but often coursework which has received a percentage of teacher guidance must receive reduced marks. Try to choose original ideas which involve your personal experiences.

5 Vary your sources of information as much as possible. Books, magazines, leaflets and catalogues will help, but do not just copy out whole chunks. You should be interpreting and using information, not just copying it. Useful sources of information can be: your school and public libraries, the local Town Hall, the post office, CAB, Consumer Advice Centre, social services department, and local shops. You can also send for information from food and toy manufacturers, clothing firms, voluntary societies, etc. Always include a stamped addressed envelope.

6 The length of a piece of work is not as important as the quality of the work. An investigation or child study which is bulky because it is full of repetitive information, magazine cuttings and unrelated pictures will not get many marks. It is your interpretation and understanding of information which the examiner is looking for. Choosing expensive fabrics or materials for an item which you make will not give you extra marks; it is suiting the material to the purpose which is important.

7 Choose a variety of methods of recording your information, such as: a written diary of events; tabulated notes; pie charts, line graphs, stick charts, bar charts; surveys; diagrams; maps; market research; experiments; questionnaires; drawings, pictures and illustrations; photographs; scrap books. You may record work on tape or make a video. Items of work being made can be photographed at various stages.

All these methods add interest to your work, and they help to show that you can make use of modern technology.

8 Do your summing up and evaluation very clearly. The item you have made should, if possible, be used by a child and its value assessed by you. It does not matter if your item is not 'as new' when sent for assessment as long as your explanation is clear. Your evaluation should show how successful your investigation or item has been and how it could be improved.

9 Do not leave your coursework until the last minute to complete. You may panic and be unable to give a satisfactory conclusion to your work. Often the summing up, critical appraisal or evaluation is allocated as many marks as the execution of the piece of coursework.

10 Present your work neatly in a folder or container. Make sure it is clearly marked with your name and examination number and the name of your school.

Examples

Investigations

1   Clearly state what the investigation is. It is usually easier if you do this in the form of a question.

2   Plan the form of your investigation and the methods you will use, such as surveys, charts, and questionnaires. Keep a list of these and have all work signed by a teacher, supervisor, official, etc., to show that it is your own work. Always date your work.

3   Carry out your plan, and make your work orderly and accurate.

4   Sum up and evaluate.

Suggestions

A   What are the best options for taking young children on holiday?

Work to be done could include:

i)   a list of all the possibilities, such as caravans, rented holiday flats, seaside hotels, holiday camps, package holidays, etc.

ii)   the advantages and disadvantages of each suggestion; comparison of suggestions; personal and family experiences.

iii)   methods and resources such as a popularity survey among families with young children; information from travel agents; bar charts of resort sunshine records; beach cleanliness investigation; day visit to a holiday camp; comparison of costs and amenities in seaside boarding houses; methods of keeping children amused on long journeys, etc.

iv)   your evaluation, including your summing up and your recommendations and suggestions for further research.

B   Is the diet of a child who mainly lives on snacks, fast foods and convenience foods as nutritious and balanced as it should be?

Work to be done could include:

i)   a definition of snacks, fast foods and convenience foods, with examples (such as:

> snacks – potato crisps, biscuits, pop, sweets, chocolate;
> fast foods – burgers, fish and chips, take-away meals;
> convenience foods – frozen whole meals, canned fruit and vegetables, dried milk);

an outline of the NACNE recommendations; the nutritional requirements for young children in chart form; the nutritive value of some of these foods, such as a packet of crisps, a Big Mac, a can of baby food; information about the dangers of food additives.

ii) methods and resources such as: a survey of the favourite foods of a group of children at a playgroup; making a meal for a child from fresh ingredients and comparing the cost and popularity with a similar convenience meal; taping interviews with children about their reactions to a Kentucky Fried/MacDonalds/Pizza House meal; a line graph of child-growth now and twenty years ago.

iii) your evaluation, summing up your results and possibly suggesting that fast foods, with the addition of some fresh foods, can be perfectly adequate.

Item for a child

1   Select an item to make which is not too advanced for your level of skills.

2   Identify a need or a problem and show how your item will solve this need or problem.

3   Consider the restrictions which the problem imposes, and adapt your item accordingly.

4   Select materials, methods of making, design, pattern and desired finished result to make the item suitable for its purpose.

5   Keep a careful, dated record of your work at all its stages, possibly in the form of a scrapbook, to include: samples of materials used, pattern, design, photographs, drawings, etc.

6   Allow the item to be used, assess its value and suggest how it could be improved or modified.

Suggestions

A   Design and make a toy suitable for a six-month-old baby with a partial visual handicap.

The *aims* of the toy are to give pleasure and to help with development.

The *restrictions* include: the visual handicap; a six-month-old baby being unable to walk or talk; being aware of safety, etc.

i) **Choice**
What could you make? A soft toy would be suitable.
How could you make it suitable for a visually handicapped baby?
A soft-textured ball with a bell inside would be a good selection.

ii) **Materials**
Which fabrics are soft, feel nice, and have different textures? How can they all be included?
Fur fabric, brushed cotton, any material with a looped pile, velvet, and satin would be suitable. Make the ball in sections and use different fabric for each section.

iii) **Design**
How can the ball be made to have a pleasant noise?
You could put inside it bells, dried peas in a sealed cardboard container, or a musical toy.

iv) **Construction**
Safety is very important. Seams must be strong – sew by machine; use a firm material as stuffing; stitch the opening up firmly; do not have external decorations which can be pulled off.

v) **Evaluation**
Visit a visually handicapped child in a playgroup or special unit, or one personally known. Does the toy work – does the child like it?

B Design and make an item which would help to develop the social skills of a 4–5-year-old child.

The *aims* of the item are to give the child practice with the social skills he or she will require at school.

The *restrictions* include: child's manual dexterity not yet fully developed; muscular co-ordination still quite restricted; short span of interest.

i) **Choice**
What could you make?
A board or a book with a selection of activities which will give practice with social skills, such as a felt shoe outline with a shoe lace; a button and buttonhole; a zip fastener; the child's name in raised letters.

ii) **Materials**
Fabrics which are firm but pliable, have non-fray edges, and are colourful. Suggestions include felt, heavy iron-on vilene, wooden board covered with an easy-grip surface.

iii) **Design**
Assess the advantages of the item being a book or a board. How can the activities be applied firmly? Consider making the item attractive to a child. The problems of safety, strength, hygiene and cost must be studied.

iv) **Construction**
How will the pages of the book be constructed? Will the activity be stitched or stuck to the backing?

v) **Evaluation**
How does the item stand up to active play? Are the children interested? Do any parts come loose? Is it too heavy or unmanageable? Could it be improved?

These suggestions for practical work and investigation are not intended to offer complete instructions, but just to give you some guidelines to work within.

APPENDIX D   Assessment Objectives

The following assessment objectives link with those of the GCSE national criteria for Home Economics.

SECTION A   The family in society

i   To define the structure of family patterns and the changes in those patterns.

ii To record the factors which have helped to bring these changes about.

iii To describe the effects of changing circumstances upon family life.

iv To assess and evaluate the effects of changing family life within present-day society.

SECTION B   The family background

i   To define the composition of the family and distinguish between family relationships.

ii To identify the responsibilities of parenthood and analyse the pressures on family life and their effects on the modern family.

iii To distinguish cause, effect and treatment relevant to wrong-doing against society.

iv To study aspects of income and family spending and assess the effects of poverty.

v   To identify buying patterns and evaluate the efficiency of consumer laws.

SECTION C   Handicapped children and their families

i   To identify the common physical and mental handicaps which affect children, the causes of these handicaps, and their possible prevention.

ii To record the needs of handicapped children and their families.

iii To describe statutory and voluntary treatments and help available, and how to obtain these provisions.

iv To assess and evaluate the various courses of action and sum up their effectiveness.

SECTION D   **Community care and provision**

    i To specify the statutory legislation and rights relating to community care.

   ii To record and evaluate the social services and health benefits available in the UK.

  iii To discuss and assess voluntary work and organisations.

Glossary

This gives an explanation of some of the terms used in this book.

A
ALTERNATIVE FAMILY Alternatives to the natural family, e.g. foster parents
ANTISOCIAL Unacceptable behaviour
ARRANGED MARRIAGE A marriage in which a spouse is chosen by the parents of a girl or boy for her or him
AT-RISK REGISTER A list of children considered to be in need of the supervision of a social worker

C
CHILD-CENTRED FAMILY A family in which children are given major importance
CHRONIC Long-term, long lasting
COMMUNE A unit of people living together, sharing their possessions
COMMUNITY POLICING Bringing the police into contact with the public
CONJUGAL FAMILY A nuclear family
CONSUMER PROTECTION Helping people who purchase goods
CONURBATION A continuous built-up area
CRIMINAL FAMILIES Families with a continuous history of crime

D
DEPRIVED AREA An area which is run down and lacking amenities
DOUBLE DEPRIVATION Depriving a child of natural parents and then of foster parents or other alternative family
DUAL STANDARDS Having one set of rules for parents and different ones for children

E
EGOCENTRIC Thinking only of oneself
ENRICH To add to
ENVIRONMENT Surroundings
ENVIRONMENTAL HEALTH Aspects of health affected by factors in the environment
ETHNIC MINORITY GROUPS Groups of people whose racial and cultural origin differs from that of most of the society they live in

I

ILLEGAL DRUGS   Potentially dangerous drugs not prescribed by a doctor, or on sale from an unauthorised supplier
IMMIGRANT   A person who comes to one country from another
INTEGRATION   Unifying, making into a whole
INTERRELATED HANDICAPS   Two or more handicaps suffered together
INTROVERTED   Turned in on oneself, withdrawn

L

LATCH-KEY CHILDREN   Children who are given a key to let themselves into the home on a regular basis because no adults are there when they get home
LIAISON   Getting together; communication between groups

M

MALNUTRITION   Lack of adequate nourishment, resulting from an incomplete diet
MANUAL WORKER   A person who works with his or her hands, usually at an unskilled or semiskilled level
MARITAL   Relating to marriage
MATERIALISTIC   Concerned only with possessions and ignoring spiritual values
MEDIA   Agencies involved in supplying information, e.g. TV, magazines, newspapers

N

NEW TOWNS   Post-war towns which have been purpose built, e.g. Milton Keynes
NON-CUSTODIAL TREATMENT   Sentences which do not require serving a prison sentence, e.g. probation

P

PERINATAL   Delivery and birth period
PERMISSIVE SOCIETY   A society which allows excessive freedom of conduct
POLLUTION   Making harmful living conditions, contaminating
PRIMARY HEALTH CARE   Doctors, dentists, opticians, etc. who are in the front line of health care
PROBATION   Non-custodial treatment of an offender

R

RECESSION   A temporary decline or setback
RECONSTITUTED FAMILY   A family formed by spouses who divorce and then marry another partner
REHABILITATION   To retrain, make a fresh start
RETARDED DEVELOPMENT   Development which is slowed down by external factors
ROLE REVERSAL   Traditional jobs or duties being undertaken by the other partner, e.g. fathers caring for children
RURAL COMMUNITY   A group of people living in the countryside, e.g. a village

S

SEDENTARY WORKERS 'Sitting down' workers, e.g. office workers
SENSORY To do with the senses
SEXUAL ABUSE The ill-treatment of children in a sexual way
SIBLINGS Brothers and sisters
SOCIALISATION Integrating into the community; mixing in
SOCIAL SKILLS The habits needed for living in a society, e.g. acceptable eating habits
SOCIOECONOMIC GROUPINGS People grouped according to the work performed and income received
SOCIOLOGIST Someone trained in sociology who studies human society and culture
SOLVENT ABUSE Using solvents for the wrong purpose, e.g. glue-sniffing
SPOUSE A husband or wife
STATUS Social position

U

URBAN AREA A town or city area
URBANISATION Giving an area the qualities and characteristics of a town

Index